Burlesque Humor Revisited

A History-like Comedy Run-down from the World of Burlesque Condensed into Twelve Classic Sketches

by Dick Poston

A SAMUEL FRENCH ACTING EDITION

New York Hollywood London Toronto
SAMUELFRENCH.COM

Copyright © 1977 by Dick Poston

ALL RIGHTS RESERVED

CAUTION: Professionals and amateurs are hereby warned that *BURLESQUE HUMOR REVISITED* is subject to a Licensing Fee. It is fully protected under the copyright laws of the United States of America, the British Commonwealth, including Canada, and all other countries of the Copyright Union. All rights, including professional, amateur, motion picture, recitation, lecturing, public reading, radio broadcasting, television and the rights of translation into foreign languages are strictly reserved. In its present form the play is dedicated to the reading public only.

The amateur live stage performance rights to *BURLESQUE HUMOR REVISITED* are controlled exclusively by Samuel French, Inc., and licensing arrangements and performance licenses must be secured well in advance of presentation. PLEASE NOTE that amateur Licensing Fees are set upon application in accordance with your producing circumstances. When applying for a licensing quotation and a performance license please give us the number of performances intended, dates of production, your seating capacity and admission fee. Licensing Fees are payable one week before the opening performance of the play to Samuel French, Inc., at 45 W. 25th Street, New York, NY 10010.

Licensing Fee of the required amount must be paid whether the play is presented for charity or gain and whether or not admission is charged.

Stock licensing fees quoted upon application to Samuel French, Inc.

For all other rights than those stipulated above, apply to: Samuel French, Inc.

Particular emphasis is laid on the question of amateur or professional readings, permission and terms for which must be secured in writing from Samuel French, Inc.

Copying from this book in whole or in part is strictly forbidden by law, and the right of performance is not transferable.

Whenever the play is produced the following notice must appear on all programs, printing and advertising for the play: "Produced by special arrangement with Samuel French, Inc."

Due authorship credit must be given on all programs, printing and advertising for the play.

No one shall commit or authorize any act or omission by which the copyright of, or the right to copyright, this play may be impaired.
No one shall make any changes in this play for the purpose of production.
Publication of this play does not imply availability for performance. Both amateurs and professionals considering a production are strongly advised in their own interests to apply to Samuel French, Inc., for written permission before starting rehearsals, advertising, or booking a theatre.
No part of this book may be reproduced, stored in a retrieval system, or transmitted in any form, by any means, now known or yet to be invented, including mechanical, electronic, photocopying, recording, videotaping, or otherwise, without the prior written permission of the publisher.

ISBN 978-0-573-62062-1   Printed in U.S.A.   #4710

Dedicated to

JOSIP ELIC

a very funny comic
who loaned me his collection
of 156 burlesque sketches
from which these skits were then written.

and to

JOEY FAYE

a very funny comic
who taught me
everything I know about burlesque humor.

With much thanks.
Dick Poston

PREFACE

Hardly any of the complete, classic burlesque skits and sketches, as performed in the heyday of the stripper, ever found its way to the printed page. Most of them started out as a short, blackout idea pertaining to "the human condition" of that time—a jaundiced and satirical eye on speakeasies, marital and otherwise relationships, depression days circumstances and any and all escapist-type humor that was possible in that era of time. That blackout idea would then be enlarged upon, added to, polished and perfected—always in performance, with ad libs and improvisations, over and over—until eventually would evolve and emerge a veritable gem (often risque) of raucous (for those audiences) hilarity. And yet these turns in a burlesque show were considered merely filler between the musical and stripping numbers.

But they seem to have furnished a very solid foundation for today's humor standards. "All In the Family," "The Honeymooners," "Sanford and Son," "Barney Miller," "Laugh In" and even the plays of Neil Simon all appear to rely on a burlesque style of humor—the plays-on-words, the psychological twist, that jaundiced and satirical eye on *today's* "human condition." The twelve sketches herein have been revised, adapted and edited from a collection of 156 old-time burley skit ideas, each of which was anywhere from one-and-a-half to maybe four pages long. By up-dating, organizing, compressing and reconstructing them, "Top Banana" Joey Faye's former "Straight Man" has been able to fashion new variations of classic, old, burlesque routines. And finally these sketches have found their way to long deserved publication.

BURLESQUE HUMOR REVISITED

by

DICK POSTON

The late, Honorable Fiorello H. La Guardia, Mayor of New York City from 1934 to 1945, was not solely responsible for the unlamented demise of burlesque, no matter what anyone tells you. In fact, if any anti-burlesque laws or rulings had been passed during La Guardia's reign as Mayor, Ann Corio could not have brought back her "This Was Burlesque" in the '60's.

Burlesque in New York, as it was known and loved in the thirties and early forties, died out under the weight of a multitude of factors: a war, a gradual upgrading in entertainment tastes, rocket-soaring costs of stage presentations and, in my opinion, the development of a breed of kamikaze performers who persisted in methodically degrading burlesque down to the raunchy, the foul and eventually to the downright embarrassing. As a result, burlesque audiences peeled off in clouds of bad taste and flew away. And it was this latter day smut-burlesque that Mayor La Guardia ordered his police department to crack down on. Small wonder the burley theatres quickly went dark.

But one segment of burlesque lives on—in fact, will never die. It grows and flourishes and, with today's television tastes, gets even better and better all the time. Burlesque humor abounds, even now. Especially now. Analyze the most popular types of comedy today and they all seem to have roots in the burlesque style humor of the '20's and '30's.

To begin with, the term "burlesque humor" is a redundancy in itself. The word burlesque is derived from the Italian words, *burlesco* or *burlare* meaning to poke fun at, to ridicule, to make jest of. "Burla" and "jest" equals "burlesque." Webster's says: "To treat a serious subject ridiculously. To imitate so as to ridicule." Boiled down, burlesque humor is the ridiculous imitation of, the poking of fun at—*The Human Condition*. Remember that phrase, "The Human Condition."

For example, screen writers Woody Allen and Mel Brooks seem to have honed burlesque humor to a fine and brilliant sharpness in their wild, wonderful movies. How? By showing us that recognizable and identifiable Human Condition and then treating it for laughs.
treating it for laughs.
My own personal definition of burlesque comedy is "Mental Magic." Intellectual sleight-of-tongue manipulation. The thought twist. The word reversal, quicker than the expectation. Burlesque comedy is one's own mental agility slipping on an actually anticipated banana peel. We know we're going to be fooled verbally. We recognize and identify with the Human Condition or the semi-serious matter being ridiculed or satirized. We turn on to a burlesque-style comedian in advance and we marvel at his timing, his delivery and his gifted tickling of our emotional reflexes. And we laugh. And to put frosting on the cake the old-time burley comedian often went risque. That *Human Condition* used to be treated naughty and funny. Then they started to make it dirty and embarrassing. And *that* was the end of burlesque, the real old-time burlesque. But I said that, didn't I? At least that's this one Straight Man's opinion.

A quote from Ann Corio's marvelous picture book, "This Was Burlesque": "Burlesque first appeared in the English language in a play entitled, 'The Most Lamentable Comedy and Most Cruel Death of Pyramus and Thisbie.' Produced in London in 1600, it set the pattern for all the lusty satires and parodies to follow." Then, two hundred and some years later, according to Miss Corio, a playwright named John Brougham (in his day referred to as "The American Aristophanes") was wowing New York audiences with his burlesque renditions of current uptown dramas as well as Shakespearean classics. Then an old-time melodrama incorporating tights-adorned ballet girls and called "The Black Crook" became a famous landmark on the road toward the heyday of burlesque. Lydia Thompson brought from England her very chubby girls wearing what practically amounted to long underwear. And in the late 1800's Michael B. Leavitt combined a minstrel show, vaudeville acts and a classic, burlesque, one-act farce to inaugurate the first burlesque revue. And so the burlesque show, as it came to be known, was born. The first public sexy dance was conceded to be by "Little Egypt" at the World's Fair in Paris in 1900 and the first supposed stripper was acknowledged to be Hinda Wassu whose shoulder strap broke one night and set the male audience on its ear. Poor Hinda, so the story goes, was mortified and expected to be fired from the chorus line. Instead, they say, the theatre manager offered her more money to make sure the same shoulder strap broke every performance thereafter. I don't know those to be the true facts, I wasn't there, but that's the way the story goes. But I'm getting off the subject of burlesque comedy.

The famous comics and comedians, known today and in the recent past, who started out and/or worked in burlesque are legion: Will Rogers, Eddie Cantor, W. C. Fields, Joe E. Brown, Red Skelton, Al Jolson, Fannie Brice, Leon Errol, Bert Lahr, Bobby Clark, Ed Wynn, Jackie Gleason, Joe Penner, Buster Keaton, Jimmie Durante, Phil Silvers, Red Buttons, Danny Thomas, Rags Ragland, Gallagher and Sheehan, Smith and Dale, Abbott and Costello, Joey Faye, Bozo Snyder, Steve Mills and how many hundreds more.

There's a great weeping and wailing in the entertainment-nostalgia world these days. Check almost any T-V talk show: "The old-time burlesque sketches have all disappeared," we're told. "It's a lost art," they cry. "Those marvelous old bits and routines—gone forever—none preserved for posterity." Bushwa!

Almost every college in the country in any given year is turning out a Liberal Arts Masters Degree on some graduate student's collection of old-time burlesque and vaudeville turns. It's becoming almost a research cliché.

The claimed compilations of burlesque sketches reach to infinity. I, myself, worked with an old burley comic who says he has over 8,000 sketches stored away. I smile. Not that I disbelieve him, I just think he tends to exaggerate. I don't think there ever were 8,000 separate, individual sketches. What there are, no doubt, are about 88,000 *variations* on a hundred or so basic routines.

I've worked on several Red Skelton T-V shows and although we never discussed it, it is generally conceded that Red probably has the greatest collected library of burlesque and comedy memorabilia to be found in all the world. He's a brilliant and clever man and whatever institution inherits this valuable accumulation will have a priceless treasure indeed.

But the thing is, you see, very few old-time burlesque routines were ever written down—*the way they were performed*. A sketch could run from four or five to fifteen or twenty minutes. Some of them, in their final form, were practically one-act plays. But in all the hundreds of sketches I've read and performed in, believe me, the original content of the sketch idea—as written out to be produced and performed *from*—would fill maybe one or two, two-and-a-half pages at the most. That skeleton framework of the skit was given to the people who were to do it. And as it was presented, over and over—quite often over a hundred times a month—(they hardly *ever* rehearsed a sketch)—then the ingenuity and inventiveness and comedy flair of the burley performer would blossom forth and that one-page concept would grow and evolve and develop and become slick and polished and perfected until it barely resembled the original one or two page sketch idea. In addition, burlesque performers had no compunction whatsoever about stealing and borrowing and incorporating jokes and bits from other shows and sketches into their's and *that* finished product was what was seldom, if ever, written down.

Recently I bumped into an actor, sketch collector, Lambs Club member and friend of mine named Josip Elic. He loaned me his collection of 156 burlesque skits. As I've indicated, taken at face value, they were practically nothing. Not only were they almost impossible to read, they *were not funny*—as such. For a multitude of reasons: You can't write the timing; you can't write the "take" reactions—that goes without saying. But mostly it's impossible to read in the ad libs and own personal bits and pieces and shtick expressions that each individual comic will and always did incorporate into *his* presentation of the scene. And these ingredients made the sketch his very own. But they were just hardly ever written down. Get the picture?

Yet each sketch of one-and-a-half to two-and-a-half pages of *basic idea* reminded *me* of a joke that would fit or a gag that we used to throw in or a line or bit from some other skit that would be borrowed and tossed in.

Also the most noticeable discovery in reading over those old-time pieces was their similarity and the related categories that the sketches seemed to fall into. Ten or twelve different routines might follow one basic theme and pattern and I found that from those dozen or so skits one sketch could be fashioned that would approximate—as closely as possible on paper—the type of turn that probably evolved and developed and was incorporated into a burlesque show of forty or fifty years ago. And this I have herewith attempted to do.

A perfect example of what I mean is to be found later in "The Schoolroom Scene." It was, as I recall, a standard staple in burlesque back in the old days. But I have never seen it written down and I doubt if it ever was before now. Yet this one herein is almost totally unoriginal. With anybody. I remember Joe Yule, Sr. doing a schoolroom scene and I remember his blackout punch line. From there on one merely throws in scads of other material, shapes it, rearranges it, develops it, molds it, polishes it and the result is, hopefully, an audience pleasing gem. (We've performed it and it is.)

Another bit of alteration on my part in the material these scenes are derived from was to cut down the casts to the basic need of three. In all those one-and-a-half, two-page bits I read they referred to the First Comic, the Second Comic, the Straight Man, the Juvenile and the Character Man. On the distaff side the players were always called the Ingenue, the Soubrette and the Prima Donna. (And often as not, "Prima" was spelled with two "M"'s.) But aside from what it said in the script, the leading female in most sketches was commonly known as the Talking Lady. So for purposes of simplification I will henceforth cast these sketches as they might be performed by a "Comic," a "Straight Man" and a "Talking Lady." I can be forgiven that liberty, can't I?

While we're on the subject of nomenclature, people are always asking about the term "Top Banana." For every performer who ever worked in burlesque there is probably a different version of where the term came from. Some claim it was born in an old skit, "The Three Bananas," referring to actual prop bananas, not people. But like most burley terms and old-time carney terms the expression probably just happened. Who first said, "Who's the chief honcho around here?", Captain John Smith or some Madison Avenue copywriter? Same damn thing.

I'm just sort of rambling along here and I don't know if I'm being very helpful or informative for you or not.

I suppose I could sort of go a bit more into detail on what I mean by the "style" of burlesque comedy—the timing, the delivery, the reacting. For example, the reactions: Most everyone knows what a "take" is. There is all manner of "takes." The stumble take, the double and triple takes, the skull, the slow burn, etc., etc. Lou Costello and Jack Benny and Johnny Carson have perfected the "deadpan stare" take. Mary Tyler Moore is very good at it, too. And maybe this is the place to say what, to most of us, is at once self-evident that there are two kinds of comedy reaction: the imitated and innovative. And almost all innovated is partially imitated. This can't be helped. Because burlesque style humor can never be thoroughly explained nor out-and-out taught, as such. It has to be discovered and developed almost by osmossis. The only truly successful teacher of burlesque comedy style is pure, on-your-feet experience. Thousands of words can be said and written trying to illustrate and teach it and it won't scratch the surface. You've got to *watch* it, *sleep* yourself in it, and then *do* it. And do it and do it and *do* it some more! Then you add your own coloring, your own interpretation and listen for the laugh. You get it and next time maybe you embellish it or maybe tone down to improve it. What kind of laugh does *that* bring? Then try it another way. And another. Changes ever so subtle. And on and on and on.

Burlesque comedians are not born. Even a burlesque style comic who never played burlesque or maybe never even saw it probably was "that funny kid in high school" who loved old Marx Brothers and W. C. Fields and Laurel and Hardy movies and incorporated imitations of them and their burlesque and semi-burlesque styles into his school hall antics. Gradually, over the years of performing, performing, performing—everything from breaking them up in the locker room to putting lamp shades on his head at parties,—the embryonic comedian developed a style of comedy delivery and that style's original seed was probably planted someplace way back in burlesque.

I've tried to teach it, you know. I took a handful of serious college student actors and comedians. I gave them the words and showed them the moves. I pounded in the timing—quick here, pause there, wait, take, staccato comeback, slow burn, bring in the audience, aghast reaction, frustration, screaming pseudo-hysteria, wide-eyed disbelief, etc., etc. You know who ended up most frustrated? Me. After long, patient explanations—after beaucoup demonstrations—And they'd *laugh!* Oh, they loved it. Great appreciators. They wanted desperately to be able to carbon copy it all. But it just doesn't happen like that. They'd often get a hint of it. There'd be tinges of burlesque comedy flair and it would be evident that with time and experience they'd pick it up and fashion the style to themselves. Which gives hope. But it also shows that the development of a burlesque humor style takes time, dedication and *practice*. An awful lot of in-front-of-a-live-audience practice.

And burlesque humor is never quite like experimental theatre or theatre of the absurd where the audience is mostly an interpreter and practically as much the creator as the artist on stage. In burlesque the performers are strictly the communicators and the audience is strictly the communicatee. As Arnold Stang once told me, "There is a purity in burlesque comedy."

One thing about some burlesque-style comics that is at the same time a strength and also a weakness was/is their lack of comedic dimension or versatility. Above and beyond the worth of their material this shortcoming can often times stamp them as distinctly different and uniquely individual. And today it can also sometimes prompt a monotony-yawn. The good comedians—I mean *really* good, by today's standards—are the ones who can vary their skills in and with diverse and yet always funny characterisations. Red Skelton, for example, has a whole stock company full of characters he can portray. Jackie Gleason stretches out beyond "And away we go!" And they are able to immerse themselves into those characters that they enact and give us variety and dimension. Others, like Milton Berle and Flip Wilson and Carol Burnett, for example, give themselves other characters to portray in scenes, yes, but they're still pretty much the same two-dimensional, burlesque-style comic in all of them. A little bit of Phil Silvers and Jerry Lewis can go a long way. They are good, of course— very funny and deservedly popular—but, for some, they can wear a mite thin after a while. And though this may seem blasphemy, even Lou Costello and W. C. Fields could, in my opinion, too often be too much a pair of cardboard comics.

On the other hand, some burlesque comedians—some you may never have heard of—were/are merely terrific. The greatest I ever knew or worked with was a sweet, sweet guy, the late Irving Harmon; so subtle, so appealing, so fantastically believable in whatever character he portrayed. He could be

Charlie Chaplin, Emmett Kelly and Mickey Rooney all rolled into one. An excellent comic named Frank Silvano, former Straight Man now turned comedian, is a hilarious *comedy actor*, out touring now in his and Will B. Able's own burlesque-type revival they call "Baggy Pants Revue." Another exceptional burlesque-style comedy actor is Cliff Norton. And then there's that other very funny former Straight Man, the great Jack Albertson.

Because the thing is, you see, today's audiences seem to have a lower threshold of tolerance for raucous slapstick than in the old Ed Wynn, Buster Keaton, Bert Lahr days. They seem to require more depth in their burlesque-style comedians. I doubt if (not counting the natural nostalgia-appeal) even the exceptional Olsen and Johnson could hold a show together for very long with today's exacting audiences. The fans and critics more or less demand a funny *actor* doing their burlesque-style humor and comedies. Neil Simon mostly writes almost pure burlesque humor. But if a broad, mugging, shtick-booting burley comic of the old days tried to chew up the stage with some of his material the audiences, I feel sure, would drift out of the theatres in droves. Which is why, I believe, he is played by exceptional comedy *actors* like Walter Matthau and Jack Lemmon and Peter Falk. And still, let's face it, the comedy material itself is primarily rollicking burlesque humor.

Well, hell. Enough of my own personal, no-foundation suppositions, let's get on to the sketches.

Oh. Want to read a couple of burlesque stories? Jack Albertson, one of burley's greatest hoofers and Straight men tells this one:

"When I was a young sprout my grandfather told me never to go near a burlesque show. He warned me, 'If you go into a burlesque theatre you'll see something you *hadn't ought to see!*' Well, you know young kids; he merely whetted my curiosity. So I climbed the outside fire escape of the theatre, sneaked inside, laid low until the show started and then popped up in a seat up in the balcony. And you know something, my grandfather was one hundred percent right; I saw something I hadn't ought to see. I saw my grandfather sitting two rows in front of me a-stomping and a-whistling and carrying on something fierce."

"Top Banana," Joey Faye claims this one is true but I kind of doubt it. (Like his name, Joey Faye. In reality he's a very funny Italian named Joseph A. Paladino.) Joey says: "When I first decided to quit the Amateur Shows and the Borsht Belt resort hotels in the Catskill Mountains to go into burlesque, I told my Mom. And such a *geshrei* you never heard in all your life. She yanked me and my father and my grandparents into the front parlor and set up a holler that echoed from many neighborhoods away. 'My little boy!' she wailed. 'Going into burlesque! Why? What have I done to deserve this? *Burlesque!* With the drinking and the partying and the naked girls and the late nights and the orgies—!' And my father's plaintive voice coming from the back of the room, 'Take me! Take me!'"

Anyway—

As we go along here, bringing you these sketches—or should I say these condensations and bits of 156 sketches—I'll try to fill you in on other opinions and facts and pieces of burlesque comedy history that I've gleaned over the years. Some of it's true. Some lies. But for me, it has never failed to be fascinating. A fantastic world, my friends. Come on, join me in it for a spell, won't you? It's a gas.

For instance—one day I decided to try to find what might have been the first, short, burlesque skit ever written, and that's going back quite a ways. I doubt if I succeeded in finding the first but listen to this: It was entitled "The Beginnings of the Mirror" and I've enlarged upon it a bit because, as first discovered, it was more just a brief blackout than a full sketch.

But wait a minute—why don't I present it all to you as I originally conceived it and as we played it—as a Two Act evening's entertainment?

The cast is three, a "Straight Man," a "Comic," and a "Talking Lady." The stage is almost bare, set up as if for a lecture with a small, movable podium or music stand down center. Far up stage in the shadows are two chairs and a stool. And the show was called "Slowly I Turned."

This Comedy is comprised of the best bits and pieces from 156 old-time burlesque skits and adapted into:

ACT I

"The Beginnings of the Mirror"
"Watt Street" and "Cleaning and Dyeing"
"The Sap and the St. Louis Kid"
"The Farmhouse Scene"
"Hold the Car"
"The Courtroom Scene"
"Cot in the Corridor " ("Crazy House")

ACT II

"The Schoolroom Scene"
"Niagara Falls" ("Slowly I Turned")
"Joe, the Bartender"
"Who's On First"

ENCORE

"Hollywood"

ACT ONE

(STRAIGHT MAN *enters carrying loose-leaf binder and crosses to lectern.*)

STRAIGHT MAN. HI. I'M .... AND IN BURLESQUE PARLANCE I'M WHAT IS KNOWN AS A STRAIGHT MAN. NOW A STRAIGHT MAN IS NOT SUPPOSED TO BE FUNNY. HE FEEDS THE COMEDIAN WHO *IS* SUPPOSED TO BE FUNNY. BUT DON'T YOU PAY ANY ATTENTION—YOU LAUGH ANYWHERE AND AT ANYONE YOU WANT TO. (*Opens loose-leaf binder on lectern.*) NOW I'M GOING TO GIVE YOU A FEW FACTS AND A COUPLE OF OPINIONS ON BURLESQUE COMEDY HERE THIS EVENING (AFTERNOON). AND BY WAY OF ILLUSTRATION WE'RE GOING TO PERFORM IN A FEW OLD-STYLE BURLESQUE SKETCHES. WE HOPE TO ENTERTAIN YOU AS WELL AS BE INFORMATIVE. TO BEGIN WITH, THE TERM "BURLESQUE HUMOR" IS A REDUNDANCY IN ITSELF. BURLESQUE COMES FROM THE ITALIAN WORD, "BURLARE" OR "BURLESCO" MEANING TO LAUGH AT, MAKE FUN OF, TO RIDICULE. QUOTE: "TO TREAT A SERIOUS SUBJECT RIDICULOUSLY. TO IMITATE SO AS TO RIDICULE." UNQUOTE. YOU NOTICE, SO FAR I HAVEN'T MENTIONED SEXY, DANCING GIRL EVEN ONCE. STRIPPERS ARE A BURLESQUE WORLD APART. ANOTHER LECTURE. WE'RE GOING TO CONFINE OUR INTERESTS

HERE, THIS EVENING (THIS AFTERNOON) TO THE COMEDY. THE RIDICULOUS IMITATION OF—THE POKING OF FUN AT—*THE HUMAN CONDITION.* REMEMBER THAT PHRASE, "THE HUMAN CONDITION." LIKE—THE WAY IT IS, MAN. IT ALL STARTED, THEY SAY, WITH A GREEK WRITER NAMED ARISTOPHANES. AROUND 400 B. C. AND IT'S ALL AROUND US STILL, TODAY. "ALL IN THE FAMILY," "THE HONEYMOONERS," "SANFORD AND SON," "DEAN MARTIN," "LAUGH IN." THE HUMAN CONDITION—TREATED FOR LAUGHS. WATERGATE. SOME FUNNY. I HAD TO SAY THAT, DIDN'T I? (*The* TALKING LADY *and the* COMIC *enter from the wings and walk to the* STRAIGHT MAN *center. They stop on either side of him. He turns to look at them, puzzled.*) SOMETHING WRONG?

COMIC. NO. (*Beat.*) WE WERE JUST SAYING BACK THERE—

TALKING LADY. (*Simultaneously.*) WE'VE DECIDED THAT YOU— (STRAIGHT MAN *turns to look at each one.*)

COMIC. WE DON'T LIKE YOUR LECTURE.

STRAIGHT MAN. (*Flustered.*) WELL, I'M—SORRY TO HEAR THAT. (*Reading.*) MY OWN PARTICULAR DEFINITION OF BURLESQUE COMEDY IS MENTAL MAGIC.

TALKING LADY. WE THINK YOU OUGHT TO SKIP THE LECTURE. IT SLOWS DOWN THE SHOW.

STRAIGHT MAN. NO, NO, IT *IS* THE SHOW. (*Reading.*) SLEIGHT OF TONGUE MANIPULATION—A PLAY ON WORDS—

Comic. THE SKETCHES ARE THE SHOW. LET'S JUST DO THE SKETCHES.

Straight Man. BUT I HAVE TO—LOOK, YOU'RE NOT SUPPOSED TO BE OUT HERE, YET. I HAVEN'T INTRODUCED YOU.

Talking Lady. GO AHEAD.

Straight Man. (*Looks at them—a beat.*) THIS IS ...., OUR TALKING LADY AND ...., OUR COMIC.

Comic. HI.

Straight Man. (*Reading.*) BURLESQUE HUMOR IS YOUR OWN MENTAL AGILITY—

Talking Lady. (*To* Straight Man.) COME OVER HERE.

(*The* Talking Lady *pulls the* Straight Man *to the right. The* Comic *takes the lectern and notebook to stage left.*)

Straight Man. (*Crossing to* Comic.) HEY, WAIT A MINUTE, WHERE ARE YOU GOING? GIVE ME BACK MY LECTURE.

(*The* Comic *flips pages and points.*)

Comic. START THERE.

Straight Man. BUT WHAT ABOUT—

Comic. RIGHT THERE.

Straight Man. (*Annoyed—hesitant.*) ONE DAY I DECIDED TO TRY TO FIND WHAT MIGHT HAVE BEEN THE *FIRST* SHORT, BLACKOUT, BURLESQUE SKETCH EVER WRITTEN AND THAT'S GOING BACK QUITE A WAYS. I DOUBT IF I FOUND THE FIRST BUT LISTEN TO THIS: IT WAS ENTITLED "THE BEGIN-

NINGS OF THE MIRROR." THE SCENE IS IN A GARDEN. THE CAST, IT SAYS, QUOTE, "ARE DRESSED AS ROMANS." PROPS: A HAND MIRROR, LYING ON THE GROUND— (COMIC *and* TALKING LADY *have exited.* STRAIGHT MAN *takes a small hand mirror and lays it almost center stage.*) HMM-M? LIKE SO—

(STRAIGHT MAN *gestures to right and* COMIC *enters.* STRAIGHT MAN *exits left.*)

The Beginnings of the Mirror

(COMIC *enters in a mood of happiness and joy.*)

COMIC. Oh, what a gorgeous day! Look at that glorious sun. 'Tis simply a wonderful, beautiful—a truly marvelous day! (*Sees mirror on ground—reacts.*) Uh-oh! What is that that glistens so in the sun? A frame of sorts. Oh, ho—'tis something evil, I'll wager; 'twill bring trouble. (*Looks around furtively.*) I shall look and observe what it is. (*Looks in mirror, then puts it aside—big reaction.*) Ahh-h-h! 'Tis the face of my poor, departed father!

STRAIGHT MAN. (*He enters from left.*) Enter the wife. (*He points to stage right.*)

TALKING LADY. (*She enters right,* STRAIGHT MAN *exits left.*) What hast thou there?

COMIC. (*Hiding mirror.*) What hast who where?

TALKING LADY. Thou. There. Inside thine toga.

COMIC. 'Tis nothing, nothing at all, my dear.

TALKING LADY. It must be something.

COMIC. 'Tis nothing but an itch. I slept with the boss last night.

STRAIGHT MAN. (*He enters left and steps down to footlights.*) Excuse me. (*To Audience.*) God knows what that means. It was in the script. I assume it was meant to be funny. Ha, ha! (*Nothing—shrugs—turns to* COMIC.) Carry on.

COMIC. Get out of here!

(STRAIGHT MAN *exits left.* COMIC *and* TALKING LADY *go back into the scene.*)

TALKING LADY. Let me see it. I must see it. Why are you so anxious to hide it.

COMIC. 'Tis nothing, I swear. 'Tis but a frame I found. Have a care, it might be evil.

TALKING LADY. (*She looks at mirror hands it aside and falls back, clutching her throat.*) Agh-h-h! You wretch! 'Tis a *woman!* You deceiver! You cheat!

COMIC. No, no! 'Tis the face of my poor, departed father! (*Takes mirror—looks—holds aside.*) There! See?

TALKING LADY. You trifler! You cheat! (*Takes mirror.*) Look! 'Tis the face of a woman! (*Looks—holds aside.*) And such an ugly face. Ugh! How could you?

COMIC. 'Tis not, I tell you. (*Snatches mirror.*) Would I deceive my wife whom I love? 'Tis but the face of my dear father.

STRAIGHT MAN. (*Entering left.*) And what, may I inquire, is all this rumpus about? What are you children fighting about?

TALKING LADY. Oh, Daddy! You were so right! My husband is a philanderer! A cheat! A deceiver! A trifler! A wretch!

COMIC. I'm not, I swear!

TALKING LADY. He carries about with him a frame

containing the face of a woman. And I, his wife have *caught him!*

COMIC. Not so, dear father-in-law. On my word. I found this frame containing the face of my poor, departed father.

STRAIGHT MAN. Let me have it. Maybe I can help settle your argument. (*Takes mirror—looks—puts aside, then laughs.*) You foolish children. What fools thou art to fight so about such as this. And thou are both wrong. 'Tis but the face of a *jackass!*

TALKING LADY—COMIC—STRAIGHT MAN. (*Simultaneously.*) Bl-l-ackout!

(STRAIGHT MAN *returns to his lectern.* TALKING LADY *steps to one side and waits.* COMIC *turns up stage to get the stool and chairs.*)

STRAIGHT MAN. (*To Audience.*) And if you need proof that that sketch is old, they spelled "philanderer" with an "F."

COMIC. (*Stops and turns.*) What the hell does that prove?

STRAIGHT MAN. (*Turning pages.*) Just—shut up.

COMIC. (*Placing stool, then chairs on both sides of stool.*) I hope a black cat runs up your alley.

TALKING LADY. Now, fellas!

STRAIGHT MAN. (*Reading from notebook.*) In the late 1800's Michael B. Leavitt—

COMIC. (*Interrupting.*) Ah, ah, ah, ah!

AUTHOR'S NOTE:

Here I'd like to interrupt a bit myself. For the sake of chronology I'm now going to insert a pair of old-time vaudeville-style gems in order to build up to the way in which burlesque humor originally evolved.

Toward the turn of the century, the 1890's, one of Mister Michael Leavitt's copiers in the presentation of burlesque revues was Ada Richmond. And along came Lew Weber and Joe Fields, the most famous dialect comics of their day, specializing in Irish, German and Dutch. Later they had their own vaudeville theatre, the Weber and Fields Theatre, and the thing I think is most commendable—they never resorted to dirty. They based their humor on mala-props, spoonerisms, plays-on-words, expressions, accents and dialects. *"The Human Condition"*—in America—as it might be explained and illustrated humorously by newcomers to our shores. Weber and Fields etched an indelible chapter in the history of burlesque comedy.

Combining two of their many famous skits, here is a sample with "Watt Street" and "Cleaning and Dyeing."

Watt Street and Cleaning and Dyeing

(COMIC *and* STRAIGHT MAN *enter from opposite sides and greet each other "in one."*)

COMIC. Ha, Meyer!
STRAIGHT MAN. Adolph, my friend. Ach, so good to see you. How are you?
COMIC. So, I'm not so good. You know how *nervous* I am.
STRAIGHT MAN. Tsk, tsk, tsk! Such a shame. You've got to take it easy.
COMIC. (*Frightened and nervous.*) Who?
STRAIGHT MAN. You.
COMIC. (*Looking behind him.*) T-t-take what?
STRAIGHT MAN. (*Soothing.*) You've got to be calm, Adolph.
COMIC. Yes! That's right. I've got to be calm. (*Relaxing.*) Calm. Calm. Calm. Say, what are you doing in this neighborhood?
STRAIGHT MAN. Well, I work in this neighborhood.
COMIC. You *do?*
STRAIGHT MAN. Why, yes.
COMIC. I didn't know that. Tell you what—you're the only man I know who doesn't make me nervous. So you tell me where you work, I'll come and pick you up and we'll go have lunch together.
STRAIGHT MAN. That will be wonderful!
COMIC. So tell me the street you work on, I'll come and pick you up.

STRAIGHT MAN. Watt Street.

COMIC. The street you work on. So I come pick you up, we go have lunch.

STRAIGHT MAN. Watt Street.

COMIC. The street that you're working on.

STRAIGHT MAN. Watt Street.

COMIC. The street where you work.

STRAIGHT MAN. Watt Street.

COMIC. (*Nervously.*) Why won't you tell me what street you work on?

STRAIGHT MAN. I'm telling you.

COMIC. You're not telling me, you're *asking* me!

STRAIGHT MAN. Oh, I see. Look, when I say "Watt Street," I don't mean *"What* street?", I mean, "Watt Street."

COMIC. Ohh-h-h— Look, when I say you're crazy, I don't mean you're insane, I mean you're *nuts!*— that's what you are.

STRAIGHT MAN. Now take it easy. Be calm.

COMIC. Okay, I'm calm. I'm calm, I'm calm. Now look: everything has a name.

STRAIGHT MAN. That's right.

COMIC. The country has a name. The state has a name. The city has a name.

STRAIGHT MAN. It certainly does.

COMIC. *You* have a name. I can't say what it is— there's nice people out there, but *you have a name* and—and— (*Wagging finger, getting excited.*)

STRAIGHT MAN. Now take it easy—

COMIC. Okay, I'm calm, I'll be calm. Now—tell me the name of the street you work on.

STRAIGHT MAN. Watt Street.

COMIC. No, no, no, I can't stand it!

STRAIGHT MAN. Now, Adolph, please. Look, I work on Watt Street—W-A-T-T, Watt Street.

Comic. Oh, *Watt* Street! Why didn't you say so?
Straight Man. I did. I work in a dry cleaning shop.
Comic. I thought you were funnin' me.
Straight Man. Naw-w—
Comic. You got a good job?
Straight Man. Pretty good.
Comic. What are you doing?
Straight Man. I'm dyeing.
Comic. (*Slow, blinking take.*) You look good.
Straight Man. I feel pretty good.
Comic. (*Pointing finger.*) You're starting again.
Straight Man. After all, if I don't dye, I can't live.
Comic. You're starting again!
Straight Man. And if I don't live, I can't dye. (*Laughs.*)
Comic. (*Frustration.*) Um-m—hm-m—hm-m! Look, look,—eight o'clock, I'm sick.
Straight Man. Aw-w—
Comic. Nine o'clock, I die.
Straight Man. Oh, you can't dye.
Comic. I *can't—die!??*
Straight Man. You don't belong to the union.
Comic. I have to belong to a union to *die??*
Straight Man. Ooh-h-h—You want to dye a *scab?*
Comic. I'll die any way I *want* to!
Straight Man. You may dye, but we wouldn't recognize you! (*Starts to turn away.*)
Comic. (*Jumping up and down, following after.*) If I die, you'll recognize me!
Straight Man. (*Heading for the wings.*) No, no, no. We never recognize non-union dyers. (*Both rave to off.*)
Comic. (*Very excited.*) You're going to tell me how to die! I'll die any way I want to! Who do you think you are—you're talking to—? (*Both exit.*)

AUTHOR'S NOTE:

Frustration. The Comic in a quandary. One of the most popular categories of burlesque humor and burlesque sketches. Get the picture? Remember the classic sketch, "Flugle Street?" The poor schlemiel trying to find his way to the Paskuniak Hat Company with all the nuts and zanies he meets on Flugle Street giving him nothing but a hard time.

Okay. Now let's move on. The following sketch sounds like it goes back to the '20's. But if you tune your ear to the late 30's and early 40's you can almost hear the Straight Man doing a take-off on Bogart or Cagney.

I remember seeing versions of this that were big productions, veritable one-act plays with a large cast, a musical combo on stage, B-girls, a bouncer-bartender, a crooked cop (In a speakeasy? Of course.) and the Talking Lady even sang a torch song. The thing is, see, burlesque performers loved to satirize and do comedy take-offs on heavy melodrama. In fact they leaned pretty heavily on it. Otherwise known as "the clown who wanted to play Hamlet."

Anyway, back to the show—

COMIC. (COMIC *crosses to* STRAIGHT MAN *while addressing Audience.*) Burlesque performers loved to satirize and do comedy take-offs on heavy melodrama. The following sketch sounds like it goes back to the 1920's. (*Takes* STRAIGHT MAN's *arm, pulls him away from the lectern and starts to lead him off stage.*)

STRAIGHT MAN. But wait! I'm still—I didn't—

(COMIC *continues to take* STRAIGHT MAN *into the wings. The* TALKING LADY *enters from the other side of the stage and comes down to the stool and chairs.*)

The Sap and the St. Louis Kid

(*Stool down center, chairs on each side.*)

TALKING LADY. I'm feeling so low I could play whist with a snake. I'm the moll of The St. Louis Kid and I hear he just busted out of stir. And they'll catch him again. And this time they'll send him away for life. (*Looks around at room.*) This is our old hangout, The Kit Kat Club. Lord, the memories. But he'd never dare come here. No, it's too hot. But I don't know what to do—where to go. (*Sits facing front.*) What's the use? What the hell's the use?

(*As TALKING LADY lowers her head and weeps, STRAIGHT MAN enters, sees her, looks back over his shoulder and comes down to her.*)

STRAIGHT MAN. You fixin' to buy a drink, Moll?
TALKING LADY. (*Looking up and straight out.*) That voice! That voice! (*Turns—sees him—jumps up.*) Oh, Kid! (*Runs into his arms and cries.*)
STRAIGHT MAN. Nix! Nix! Nix! Dummy up, Moll. Now it's okay. I'm glad you're here.
TALKING LADY. Oh, Kid, I've been so worried about you.
STRAIGHT MAN. Nothing to worry about. Things are gonna break for us now and soon we'll be on easy street.
TALKING LADY. (*Gasps—falls back.*) Kid! You're not going to pull any more crooked deals, are you?
STRAIGHT MAN. Now what do you mean by that? Are you trying to make a boob out of me? Okay, then scram!

TALKING LADY. Oh, Kid, I'm so sick of this! Why don't you quit and go straight?

STRAIGHT MAN. What do you mean you're sick of it? Why, trimmin' suckers in my long suit. That's what suckers was made for—for me to trim.

TALKING LADY. And then what do you get for it? You get caught and you do a stretch. Then who's the sucker and who's the wise guy? (*Cries.*)

STRAIGHT MAN. Okay, Moll, okay. I guess you're right like always. There, there, there, now. Don't take it so to heart. Why, we're not so bad. Just a couple of rolling stones. Stop crying, Molly, I'll—I'll do what you ask.

TALKING LADY. (*Looking up happily.*) Oh, Kid!

STRAIGHT MAN. (*Eagerly.*) But first we gotta have a stake to quit with, don't we? One more sucker, Moll, one more sucker and I'm cuttin' clean, I promise you. Now keep your shirt on and listen. I just steered a hick-sap down here to the Kit Kat and he's due any minute. He's got a bank roll big enough to choke a horse. But I need your help, Moll. I need your help on this one, last, easy haul, okay?

TALKING LADY. What do you mean, Kid?

STRAIGHT MAN. Oh, you know. All you gotta do is flash that pretty smile of yours and leave the rest to me. How about it, Moll? We'll trim this one boob and quit. What do you say, baby?

TALKING LADY. All right, Kid. But this is the last time.

STRAIGHT MAN. Gee, you're a regular pal, Molly. Shh! Here he comes now.

(STRAIGHT MAN *ducks away and off. The* COMIC *enters with his eyes wide and his pants legs rolled up.*

He carries an umbrella and a brown paper bag of hard candies.)

COMIC. Say, pardon me, Ma'am, is this the Kitty Kitty Club?

TALKING LADY. No, honey, this is the Kit Kat Club. Pull up a chair and park it.

COMIC. Say, that's mighty nice of you. I was looking for a Mister Kid from St. Louis.

TALKING LADY. Ha! Now there's a coincidence. The St. Louis kid is my fella. My name's Molly, what's yours?

COMIC. Jeremiah Snapgrass. How do you do?

TALKING LADY. (*Shaking his held-out hand.*) Hiya, Snappy!

COMIC. I'm from Dishpan, Arkansas. Want some lemon gundrops? (*Plops the bag of candies on the stool.*) I've only had 'em three weeks. 'Course I licked all the sugar off 'em but there's still a lot of good taste in each and every one.

TALKING LADY. No, thanks, sport. But you can buy me a drink if you want to.

COMIC. (*Surprised.*) A *drink!*

TALKING LADY. Ever have a drink before?

COMIC. Well, gosh all hemlock, o' course. I had a beer once't.

TALKING LADY. Did it go to your head?

COMIC. Nope. Went straight to my stomach. (*Laughs loudly, slaps thigh, stands and stomps around.*) I know a whole lot of good ones like that. (STRAIGHT MAN *enters and approaches.*)

TALKING LADY. I'll bet you do. Say, there's the Kid now. Hello, Kid!

STRAIGHT MAN. Hiya, Moll. Well, hello, there, Mister Snapgrass. Glad you could come down. Welcome.

COMIC. (*Standing and shaking hands.*) Howdy, Mister Kid.

STRAIGHT MAN. Moll, this is my very good friend and nothing is too good for him, understand? Whatever he wants, he gets. Get me?

COMIC. Ah, gosh. Gee, thanks.

TALKING LADY. Right, Kid. Whatever you say.

STRAIGHT MAN. So what are you two drinking?

TALKING LADY How about a whiskey?

STRAIGHT MAN. Fine.

COMIC. Got any buttermilk?

STRAIGHT MAN. Gosh, I'm afraid not, pal.

COMIC. Then I'll have a glass of hard cider.

STRAIGHT MAN. Hard cider? Can you elucidate?

COMIC. No, but I can chin myself.

STRAIGHT MAN. Hard cider. I'm afraid I can't help you there, either, partner. I'll bring two whiskeys. (*Goes.*)

COMIC. (*Reaching into pocket.*) Hope it ain't too expensive.

TALKING LADY. Ain't you got any money?

COMIC. Why, sure. I went to the bank today and made a big withdrawal. See? (*Pulls out two bills.*) Seven dollars. A one dollar bill and a six dollar bill.

TALKING LADY. (*Taking the bills.*) I'll take care of it for you, honey. I'll be the banker.

COMIC. You'll be the banker and I'll be the broker. Gimme back my money.

TALKING LADY. (*Teasing.*) And just what are you going to do with all that money?

COMIC. (*Pulling from his pocket a huge roll of bills.*) Put it with the rest of my money right here.

TALKING LADY. Twenty-three-*skiddoo!*

(Talking Lady *dazedly hands* Comic *back the two bills which he wraps around the roll and puts on the stool.* Straight Man *enters with an imaginary tray of drinks.*)

Straight Man. Here we are! (*Puts down the drinks—sees the roll.*) Well, hello, Frisco! Looky there! (*Reaches for the money on the stool.*)
Comic. (*Jumping up.*) Hold it! (Straight Man *freezes with hand held out.* Comic *tensely.*) You reach for that money, friend, and the next time you go to buy gloves you'll buy only one.
Straight Man. (*Easy.*) Oh, sure. Sorry, pal. No offense. (Comic *puts the roll in his pocket.*)
Talking Lady. Come on, Kid. Let's have this one on the house.
Straight Man. Sure thing. Why not?
Talking Lady. His intentions were good, Kid.
Straight Man. So were his father's. Drink up. (*They drink.* Comic *slowly stands, his eyes getting very wide, his mouth opening.*) Chaser?
Comic. (*Face, turning blue.*) Hell, there ain't nothing could catch it!
Straight Man. How do you like the drink?
Talking Lady. Wonderful! Oh, you Kid!
Comic. Wonderful! Oh, you hot dammit to hell! (*Pounds his chest and stamps around.*)
Straight Man. It's my own special concoction. Make it in the bathtub out back. When you're with a pretty girl, one of my drinks—you get a hug. Two drinks—you get a kiss. Three drinks—let your conscience be your guide.
Comic. You just gave my third drink first. Come here, babe.

(COMIC *reaches for* TALKING LADY *and collapses face down across the stool.* STRAIGHT MAN *takes the roll of money from his pocket.*)

STRAIGHT MAN. Okay, I got his money. Come on, give me a hand. Let's get him into the alley.

(COMIC *groans and stirs, starting to come out of it.*)

TALKING LADY. Hold your horses. He's coming to.
COMIC. (*He stands, looks around, staggers and pats his pocket. Then he gradually sobers and gets things in focus.*) Oh, so that's it. Okay. It's all right. You got me down here and you got my money. Prize sucker number one, huh? The boob from the sticks. (*Picks up his umbrella.*) Okay. It's okay. I had it coming, I guess. Except—it's not so much the money and me, it's—it's Maw and little Joey. (*Turns and starts to go.*)
TALKING LADY. Wait! Who's little Joey?
COMIC. Joey, my little brother. Maw set a heap o' love and faith in him—on a' counta his bein' a cripple. But he was always such a restless little fella. He left home one day and we didn't hear nothing from him for years. Then we learned he was here in Big Town. Barely makin' out, we heard. Maw was frettin' so about him her health started to fail. And then, on top of it all, she was losing her eyesight. There wasn't much hope for her. So Paw mortgaged the farm and sent me to try to find little Joey and bring him back to Maw so she could see him one more last time before she goes. But now—now my money's all gone and— well, now I guess I'll have to go back—back home to my dyin' Maw and tell her I—I wasn't able to find little Joey. And bring him back. For her to see once't more. (*Turns and slumps toward door.*)

TALKING LADY. No, wait! Don't go! Kid! I've been pretty rotten in my life, but not that rotten. Kid, give him back the money.

STRAIGHT MAN. You're right, Moll. Here you are, partner. I may be a crook and a slicker but I ain't never sunk that low. (*Gives roll back to* COMIC.) I had a mother once.

TALKING LADY. And here. (*Takes money from purse.*) It ain't much but it's all I got. Take this money. Find little Joey. And don't rest until you take him back to your poor, dying Maw.

STRAIGHT MAN. Here, pal. Here's over a hundred dollars. It's all I got in this world. But you take it—and welcome.

COMIC. A hundred dollars! Boy, I can sure get plenty drunk on that.

STRAIGHT MAN. No, no, no. For Joey. Use it to find little Joey and take him home to your Maw.

COMIC. Joey who?

STRAIGHT MAN. Joey *who!*

TALKING LADY. Your little brother, Joey! The crippled kid your Maw wants to see one last time!

COMIC. Oh, *that* Joey?

STRAIGHT MAN. There ain't no Joey! We been snookered! Get him!

COMIC. (*He pulls a gun and points it at them.*) Stand right where you are! Both of you. Some story, wasn't it? Not true but you fell for it. I just wanted to show you that all saps don't come from the country. So you're the St. Louis Kid? I never heard of a skunk by that name. (STRAIGHT MAN *starts for* COMIC *and stops.*) Don't try it, sucker, I'll drop you in your tracks! You brought me down here to trim, didn't you? Why, you ought to get a job in a toy store stealing pennies from little children. And you're his Moll. I thought you were mighty nice but at heart you're just like this bum. Two of a kind. Rough, tough and mean, huh? Well, I'm gonna teach you mean. I'll show you just what mean *really is!*

TALKING LADY. What—what are you going to do, Mister?

COMIC. (*Snatching bag of candies off stool.*) I'm going to take back my candy with me! (*Turns and exits.*)

TALKING LADY and STRAIGHT MAN. (*After looking at each other—to Audience.*) Bl-l—ackout!

NOTE:

Before this country went so predominantly industrial—let's say before Franklin D. Roosevelt, the union movement and all that post-depression jazz—the *Human Condition* in America included a lot more of the agrarian scene that it does today. Quite a few of our fathers, grandfathers and great-grandfathers came off the farm. Small farms.

Off the farm and into the big city on business or maybe even just for a visit, old Clem would give himself a big-city treat: he'd take in a burlesque show. Nothing like that in a Sears Roebuck catalogue. And aside from and in between watching the undressed girls, Clem saw and heard many comedians ridiculing one of those *Human Conditions*—the one to be found on a farm. Skits about the traveling salesman forced to take up lodging for the night in a farmhouse. Where he inevitably met the farmer's beautiful daughter. Or little boy.

And who enjoyed those sketches the most? Why, Clem, of course. Because, as we all know, personally identifying with a scene or situation is a tremendous asset when it comes to being entertained. As a result, "The Farmhouse Scene," for burlesque audiences, was a natural. So I've put together bits and pieces of a lot of yokel sketches to show you what I mean.

(TALKING LADY *exits.* COMIC *enters and removes stool, placing it up center.* STRAIGHT MAN *furtively crosses to his lectern.*)

STRAIGHT MAN. (*Reading.*) BEFORE AMERICA WENT SO PREDOMINANTLY INDUSTRIAL—

(COMIC *places the two chairs down stage, left of center.*)

COMIC. (*To Audience.*) The "Farmhouse Scene" was most familiar back in the glory days of burlesque comedy.
STRAIGHT MAN. Yeah, I'm getting to that. (*Reading.*) ONE OF THOSE HUMAN CONDITIONS—

(*The* TALKING LADY *enters, interrupts* STRAIGHT MAN *and walks down to the placed chairs.* COMIC *exits right.*)

The Farmhouse Scene

TALKING LADY. (*To Audience.*) Farmhouse setting. (*Pats the chairs.*) Bed. (*Indicates self.*) Farmer's daughter. (*Sits on chair.*) In the bed. (*Points to* STRAIGHT MAN.) Go!

(STRAIGHT MAN *grudgingly walks down to behind and to right of chairs.*)

STRAIGHT MAN. (*Talking to* TALKING LADY *in the bed.*) Elviry! Take your hands out from under the covers and go to sleep!

TALKING LADY. Aw, Paw! You never let me have any fun.

STRAIGHT MAN. You have lots of chores to do in the morning.

TALKING LADY. I'm tired of doing chores. I want to play sometimes.

STRAIGHT MAN. What happened to that turtle you used to play with?

TALKING LADY. He bit me.

STRAIGHT MAN. That's terrible. Musta hurt, huh? Where'd he bite you?

TALKING LADY. In the wash tub. Saturday night.

STRAIGHT MAN. By the way, where's your Maw?

TALKING LADY. She's out with the pigs. That okay with you?

STRAIGHT MAN. Hell, if the pigs don't mind, I don't care. Well, g'night, Datter.

TALKING LADY. G'night, Paw.

STRAIGHT MAN. You know, your Maw said something funny last night. I'm not sure if I understand it.

TALKING LADY. What was it, Paw?

STRAIGHT MAN. Well, you know how your two older brothers have done married and left the farm?

TALKING LADY. I know, Paw. I'm here all alone.

STRAIGHT MAN. Well, last night I said to your Maw, "Good night, mother of three."

TALKING LADY. That was sweet, Paw.

STRAIGHT MAN. And she said, "Good night, father of one." You suppose that was 'cause your brothers have done gone away?

TALKING LADY. That must be it, Paw.
STRAIGHT MAN. Well, g'night. G'night.
TALKING LADY. G'night, Paw. (COMIC *bangs on door off stage.*) What's that, Paw?
STRAIGHT MAN. Just an old woodpecker. (*Loud banging off.*)
TALKING LADY. He's a real big one, ain't he, Paw?
STRAIGHT MAN. Reckon I better answer the door. Come in!
COMIC. (*Entering.*) Howdy!
STRAIGHT MAN. Well, well, if it ain't a traveling salesman.
COMIC. You been reading my mail. How'd you know I'm a traveling salesman?
STRAIGHT MAN. 'Cause you said you was, the last time we done this sketch.
COMIC. (*Taking a swipe at* STRAIGHT MAN.) I'll give you such a k-nock! Yes, but I wasn't always a traveling salesman. Used to be a farmer from up Utah way. Are you a farmer?
STRAIGHT MAN. No, I'm a pilot.
COMIC. A pilot?
STRAIGHT MAN. Lotta manure out in our barnyard. I pile it here and I pile it there.
COMIC. Who's the Straight Man here and who's the Comic?
STRAIGHT MAN. Am I getting any laughs?
COMIC. No.
STRAIGHT MAN. You're the Comic.
TALKING LADY. (*Standing behind* STRAIGHT MAN.) Oh, Paw, he's cute.
STRAIGHT MAN. You think so? What you doin' out on a night like this, stranger?
COMIC. Tell you the truth, my car broke down.
STRAIGHT MAN. Hell you say.

Comic. And I was wonderin' if you could put me up for the night.

Straight Man. Gosh dang it all to hell, we'd sure like to. But all we got to spare is this here room and you'd have to sleep with my young daughter here.

Comic. (*Take.*) Aw, come on, is that the best you can do?

Straight Man. I'm a-feard so.

Talking Lady. (*Wriggling with anticipation.*) It's okay, Mister. I took a bath last month.

Comic. You call that hospitality? Only place you've got for me to sleep is with your beautiful, sexy, young, hot-blooded daughter here? What kind of friendliness you call that, anyway?

Straight Man. Hell, I'm sure sorry.

Comic. Well, guess I'll just have to suffer.

Talking Lady. Be you married, stranger?

Comic. Be I married! Be I *married!* Little girl, you ever hear of a Mormon. It so happens that I be a Mormon and I've got me twelve wives.

Straight Man. Hoo-o-ee! He shore be married.

Talking Lady. (*Shocked.*) Twelve wives!

Comic. Last I counted.

Talking Lady. That's awful! That's terrible! A man who'd have twelve wives ought to be *hung!*

Comic. A man with twelve wives *got* to be, honey.

Straight Man. Well, I'll say good night then, stranger. (*The* Talking Lady *jumps into "bed"—onto the chairs—squirms around and holds out her arms to* Comic. *He reaches for her.* Straight Man *turns back.*) Say, by the way, you gonna be wantin' breakfast in the morning?

Comic. (*Turning.*) Why, yes, that'll be fine.

Straight Man. Then you're gonna get it. (*Same biz*

as before. TALKING LADY *holds out arms to* COMIC, COMIC *reaches,* STRAIGHT MAN *interrupts.*) You gonna want biscuits with your breakfast?

COMIC. Why, yes, thank you.

STRAIGHT MAN. Then you're gonna get it. (TALKING LADY *holds out arms.* COMIC *stops.*)

COMIC. Hey, listen, wait a minute. Where's your paw sleep? Can he hear us? These walls seem kinda thin.

TALKING LADY. Oh, don't worry about that. Paw's deaf as a post.

COMIC. Is that right?

TALKING LADY. Can't hardly hear a thing.

COMIC. (*To* STRAIGHT MAN.) You're hard of hearing?

STRAIGHT MAN. That's right, I'm a little blind.

COMIC. I'm dubious.

TALKING LADY. (*Offering to shake hands.*) Howdy! I'm Elviry.

COMIC. No, I mean, I don't know if I believe you.

TALKING LADY. Cross my heart. Watch. (*To* STRAIGHT MAN.) Paw! Lend me five dollars!

STRAIGHT MAN. Ehh-h-h?

TALKING LADY. (*To* COMIC.) See?

COMIC. Guess you're right. I heard you perfectly.

STRAIGHT MAN. Then you lend her five dollars.

COMIC. Shove it in your ash can!

STRAIGHT MAN. Ehh-h-h?

COMIC. G'night, you horse's ancestor.

STRAIGHT MAN. G'night now. Good night. Good night.

COMIC. He sure moves slow.

TALKING LADY. Paw's been sick. Last week he was in the hospital. The doctors all said he was at death's door and I waited around all night for them to pull him through.

STRAIGHT MAN. I was breathin' my last breath. I was right up there at them golden gates talkin' to Salt Peter.

COMIC. Go on, you miserable, old— (*Shoves* STRAIGHT MAN—*turns to* TALKING LADY.) He's not sick, he's just lazy.

(STRAIGHT MAN *exits, shuffling.*)

TALKING LADY. Well, Paw ain't gonna last much longer. And when he goes he's gonna leave this whole farm to me and Maw. Maw gets this big house and I get the little house out back where we keep the sheets.

COMIC. Where you keep the what?

TALKING LADY. Where we keep the sheets.

COMIC. Oh, the sheet house! Yeah, sure. I'm starting to figure out this is quite a farm. Back home we deal mostly in crops, not so much in livestock. What do you specialize in?

TALKING LADY. Mostly we're a breedin' farm. We got us a big, old, prize bull for all the neighbors' cows.

COMIC. A prize bull, huh? I'd sure like to take a look at that bull.

TALKING LADY. You have any children, Mister?

COMIC. Do I have any children! Why, little girl, I've been married seventeen years to off-and-on twelve wives and I'm the proud father of forty-two children.

TALKING LADY. And you want to take a look at our bull?

COMIC. Yeah, I'd like to.

TALKING LADY. I want our bull to take a look at you. (*Settling on "bed"—holding out arms.*) Come on, Mister. Let's cut the palaver. Come warm me up.

(COMIC *stands grinning at* TALKING LADY, *his hands in his pockets.*)

COMIC. Warm you up?
TALKING LADY. Uh-hu. Come over here and hold me and hug me and kiss me and snuggle up to me. Hurry! Hurry! Hurry!
COMIC. (*Pleading to heaven.*) Oh, Moses, look down on your son, Cain, and make him Abel. (*Hands in pockets—hitches up pants.*)
TALKING LADY. What you doing, Mister?
COMIC. Shaking hands with the unemployed. (*Hands out of pockets—hugs and kisses* TALKING LADY.)
TALKING LADY. That's it, kiss me! Um-m-m. More! More! Kiss me!
COMIC. (*Breaking away.*) Say, you know when I was in the army forty years ago they used to put something in your coffee so's you wouldn't get all excited about girls.
TALKING LADY. They did, huh?
COMIC. I'm a son of a gun if it ain't *finally* startin' to *work!*
TALKING LADY. (*Heated—squirming on bed.*) Oh, come on, Mister, *do* something. Please me. Amuse me. Entertain me, honey.
COMIC. You mean that?
TALKING LADY. Oh, yes! Hurry! Hurry! Amuse me. Entertain me.
COMIC. Well, okay. (*Down on one knee—singing.*)
"One bright and shining light—
To show me wrong from right—"
TALKING LADY. (*Bouncing to her feet in amazed frustration—hands on hips.*) Oh, *bushwa!* (*Turns and stalks off stage.*)
COMIC. (*Following* TALKING LADY—*still singing.*) "I found in my—mother's—arms!" (*Exits.*)

NOTE:

There are dozens of versions of a basic burlesque sketch that might be referred to as "Men on the Street." Two or three men meet on a corner and banter about and relate to any one of a hundred *Human Conditions*. They're out of work or they're out of money. Or maybe they're just out of doors.

Here I've lifted sections of nine different sketches of two men on the street concerned with one universal problem: these men are out of girls. The scenes I've drawn from? Well, I used the basic framework and parts of "Hold the Car" and added parts of "Stage Door," "Love Lessons," "Tie the Shoe," "33 Dollars," "Auto Scene," "Automobile Bit," "Russian Duel" and "Seven Dollars." Plus an occasional gag or joke dredged up from a long but flawed memory.

Now in reading this you have to visualize that the Comic drags on stage with him a good-sized cardboard cut-out of a small automobile complete with a hinged door that swings out. This cut-out balances upright precariously and might easily fall down. Hence, the title.

(*The* STRAIGHT MAN *enters and crosses to his lectern. The* COMIC *enters, takes the two chairs and places them down stage, right of center, their backs to the Audience and approximately two feet apart.*)

STRAIGHT MAN. (*Reading.*) THERE ARE DOZENS OF VERSIONS OF A BASIC BURLESQUE SKETCH WE MIGHT REFER TO AS "MEN ON THE STREET." TWO OR THREE MEN MEET ON A CORNER AND BANTER ABOUT AND RELATE TO ANY ONE OF A HUNDRED *HUMAN CONDITIONS.* (*The* COMIC *exits right.*) THEY'RE OUT OF WORK. THEY'RE OUT OF MONEY. OR MAYBE THEY'RE JUST OUT OF DOORS.

TALKING LADY. (*Entering.*) These men are out of girls. (*Speaking to Audience.*) Visualize, if you will, that these two chairs represent a cardboard cut-out of a small automobile.

STRAIGHT MAN. Aw, come on! Now what are you doing?

(*The* TALKING LADY *turns to exit right. As she does, the* COMIC *enters from right, starting the scene and moving, with sound effects, to the chairs. The* STRAIGHT MAN *stands watching helplessly.*)

COMIC. Ba-room! Br-oom! Br-r-r-o-oom!

Hold the Car

(*The* COMIC *enters and moves to behind the two placed chairs, making vocal noises as if driving a powerful car.*)

Comic. Br-room! Br-r-room! Ba-a-r-r-roon! *Here*—I go down the highway a hundred miles an hour! Beep! Beep! Look out for Barney Oldfield! Br-r-*room!* Ah-*hah!* A parking space! E-e-eek! (*Backs up—parks car—positions chairs.*) Br-oom, br-oom. E-eek. Click-click. (*Steps out of car—sees* Straight Man.) Hey, ... ! What are you doing down here?

Straight Man. What do you mean, what am I—?

Comic. (*Shaking* Straight Man's *hand.*) Hiya, pal! How the hell are you? What's new?

Straight Man. (*Shaking head—then into scene.*) Well, you see, something came up.

Comic. Me, too. So I'm out looking for a girl. You know where we can find us a heifer? Br-oom! Br-oom! (*Grinds hips—scrapes feet.*)

Straight Man. Hey, hey, hey! Control yourself.

Comic. No soap—control is busted. Bring on a heifer. I'll take her down under the bridge—

Straight Man. Stop that! Now if we're going to find us a girl together she's got to be a high-class girl.

Comic. Well, it's a high-class bridge.

Straight Man. Forget the bridge.

Comic. Then we'll drive down by the side of the dam and br-oom, br-r-room, ba-a-r-*r-oom!*

Straight Man. Not by a *dam site!*

Comic. (*Take.*) I'll kick the she-lack out of you! (*Takes a swipe at* Straight Man.)

Straight Man. Watch it, there!

Comic. (*Preparing to fight.*) Come on, put up your dukes! Put 'em up! Put 'em up! (Straight Man *squares off.*) Higher! Higher! (Straight Man *raises fists—*Comic *tickles him under the arms.*) Kootchie! Kootchie! Kootchie!

Straight Man. Get the hell out of here. Anyway, I don't think you know how to treat a girl. You've got to entertain them, amuse them, keep them happy. Last night I walked a pretty girl home, I told her a funny riddle and she let me kiss her on her front stoop.

Comic. You know, I've suspected that about you for a long time.

Straight Man. You see, I entertained her.

Comic. Bet you did. What was the riddle?

Straight Man. Ah-h, let's see—oh yes, —Why is an old maid spinster like a frozen tomato?

Comic. I give up. Why is an old maid spinster like a frozen tomato?

Straight Man. Because it's—*hard to-mate-'er.*

Comic. You horse's ancestor! You asked a girl that and she let you kiss her on her front *stoop?* Why, you'll stoop to anything. Hey, I got a story that'll jolly 'em along.

Straight Man. Let's hear it.

Comic. Rudy Vallee was walking through the park. A squirrel ran up his pants leg and starved to death.

Straight Man. You can't tell that story to a lady!

Comic. Who cares about a lady? I want a heifer.

Straight Man. Now take it easy.

Comic. I'll take it any way I can get it.

Straight Man. You've got to remember, as you go through life, that in this world there's a man for every girl and a girl for every man. Now you can't improve on that.

Comic. Who the hell wants to improve on it? I just want to get *in* on it. Hey, look, did you see my car? I got me a car?

STRAIGHT MAN. You got you a car?

COMIC. (*Looking up.*) Hell of an echo in here. Yeah, I got me a car. (*Points to chairs.*) See?

STRAIGHT MAN. That's you-a car?

COMIC. Of course. What the hell do you think? That's my-a car.

STRAIGHT MAN. What kind of a car is it?

COMIC. A "Shove-her-let-her-lay."

STRAIGHT MAN. You mean a Chevrolet.

COMIC. That's what I said, a "Shove-her-let-her-lay."

STRAIGHT MAN. How's the pick-up?

COMIC. Pick-up's good. Picked up four blondes last night.

STRAIGHT MAN. Is that so?

COMIC. One of 'em had shoes on.

STRAIGHT MAN. Does it run good?

COMIC. Going up hill—not so good. Going down hill you can't keep up with the damn thing.

STRAIGHT MAN. Okay, I'm game. We'll drive around in your car and find us a girl. (*Steps into car.*)

COMIC. Hey, wait a minute, not so fast. I don't want to lose this parking space. Besides, hold it, hold it! (*Looking off stage.*) Here comes a doozy now! (*The* TALKING LADY *enters, flouncing, and stops at stage left proscenium, looking nonchalant.*) Br-oom! Br-r-room!

STRAIGHT MAN. All right, now calm down—calm down. Are you nervous?

COMIC. No, just anxious.

STRAIGHT MAN. Well, show a little restraint. Now, first we size up the situation. Now there she stands—a cute little lass.

Comic. She's got a pretty face, too. I'm sure there's enough there for the three of us.
Straight Man. Three of us?
Comic. Sure. Me, you, and then me again.
Straight Man. Now look, I don't want you to screw this up.
Comic. Not 'til we get under the bridge.
Straight Man. Forget the bridge. Now listen to me. We're going to amuse her—entertain her. We'll tell her that funny riddle.
Comic. What funny riddle? Oh, yeah, yeah, that's right.
Straight Man. But first you have to go over to her and make your peace.
Comic. Oh, hell yes.
Straight Man. Say something sweet to her.
Comic. Apple pie and honey.
Straight Man. No, no, say something endearing, something passionate. Love words that will go right *through* her.
Comic. Right. Words that will go right through her.
Straight Man. That's right.
Comic. (*Crossing to the* Talking Lady.) Prune juice.
Talking Lady. Fresh!
Comic. If it is, I'll have some.
Straight Man. No, no, no! Come over here!
Comic. I'll speak to her. I'll speak to her.
Straight Man. Like a *gentleman!*
Comic. Right. Like a gentleman. (*To* Talking Lady—*exaggerated charm.*) How do you *do-o!*
Talking Lady. (*A raucous shout.*) How do I do *what?*
Comic. (*Jumps back—to* Straight Man.) Come on, let's go find a heifer.

STRAIGHT MAN. Wait a minute—
COMIC. That one's nothing but trouble.
STRAIGHT MAN. Well, now wait a minute, hold on a second. Did you tell her the funny riddle?
COMIC. I didn't get a *chance!*
STRAIGHT MAN. Get back on over there!
COMIC. (*To* TALKING LADY.) Two old maids was lying in bed—
STRAIGHT MAN. (*Grabbing* COMIC.) No, no, no, no—
COMIC. Oh yeah, I remember—I got it. Two travelling salesmen was driving along and they saw a cow—
STRAIGHT MAN. Will you stop that! Why is an old maid like a frozen tomato?
COMIC. I give up, why is an old maid—Oh, yeah, yeah, yeah! *That's* the riddle, I got it. (*To the* TALKING LADY.) Why is an old maid's tomato frozen?
STRAIGHT MAN. No, no, no—you idiot!
COMIC. Oh, wait a minute, I got it, I got it. (*To the* TALKING LADY.) Why is an old maid like a frozen tomater? There.
TALKING LADY. I give up. Why—is an old maid—like a frozen to-*mah-toe?*
COMIC. (*Reacts.*) Get the hell out of here! How would you like to take a ride on a rusty razor blade? Now come on, say it right. Like I said it.
TALKING LADY. Oh, all right. Why is an old maid like a frozen tomater?
COMIC. Because it ain't no good in the can! (*Laughs hard—slaps thigh.*)
STRAIGHT MAN. Oh, I give up. You're hopeless. Forget the whole thing.
COMIC. What's the matter? What's wrong?
STRAIGHT MAN. You want to take a young lady for a ride in your car and you aren't even subtle! You have no finesse!

COMIC. Hot dammit to hell, I forgot the finesse. Here, hold the car. (*To the* TALKING LADY—*a raucous shout.*) Hey!

TALKING LADY. (*Right back at him.*) Wha?

COMIC. See the car?

TALKING LADY. Yeah!

COMIC. Like the car?

TALKING LADY. Yeah!

COMIC. Ever go ridin' in a car?

TALKING LADY. Yeah!

COMIC. Ever walk home?

TALKING LADY. No!

COMIC. Get in the car! (TALKING LADY *automatically crosses to car. To* STRAIGHT MAN.) You drive.

STRAIGHT MAN. How do you do? My name is .... and this is my friend, ...

TALKING LADY. Hi! I'm .... (*Starts to get in car.*) Say, that's a high step. (*With a flurry of skirt and a good deal of leg showing, steps to between the chairs.*)

COMIC. Out of the car!

(TALKING LADY "*steps high*" *to leave the car.*)

STRAIGHT MAN. What's the matter?

COMIC. (*Pointing to front row of Audience.*) That guy wasn't looking. (*To the* TALKING LADY.) Get in the car! Hold it a minute! (*Takes a notepad from pocket, drops it to floor beside car, kneels down to it and looks up to* TALKING LADY.) Get in the car!

STRAIGHT MAN. Now, what are you doing?

COMIC. (*Thumbing pages.*) Looking up her address. (*The* TALKING LADY *gets into the car with a flurry of raised skirt.* COMIC *reacts to the "view."*) Oh, there's a *full moon* tonight! (COMIC *gets into car. The* TALK-

ING LADY *stands between* STRAIGHT MAN *and* COMIC.)
Drive on, Meadows, my good man.

STRAIGHT MAN. *Here*—we go down the highway a hundred miles an hour! Beep! Beep!

COMIC. Hey, hold it! Wait a minute!

STRAIGHT MAN. What's the matter?

COMIC. We should'na left that parking space.

STRAIGHT MAN. Too late now.

COMIC. Where we going to park the car?

STRAIGHT MAN. We'll find a place.

COMIC. On a Saturday night? Every parking place is taken. Well, go ahead. Ask her.

STRAIGHT MAN. Ask her what?

COMIC. Ask her will she will or will she won't—do she do or do she don't. Let's not kid around.

STRAIGHT MAN. Well,—okay if you insist. (*To the* TALKING LADY.) My dear,—? (*Leans over and whispers.*)

TALKING LADY. Why, I don't mind if I *do-o!* (*Giggles happily.*)

STRAIGHT MAN. *Oh-h*—the sun is shining brightly in the front seat!

COMIC. (*Pleased—to the* TALKING LADY.) Come here, baby. (*Whispers in her ear.*)

TALKING LADY. Certainly *not!*

COMIC. Oh-h-h—it's raining like hell in the back seat! (*To* TALKING LADY.) Outa the car!

(*The* TALKING LADY *gets out of ther car, turns and sees* COMIC's *foot raised to her.*)

TALKING LADY. Don't you kick me! I'm a lady!
COMIC. Get back in the car, we'll find out.
TALKING LADY. Scram, buster! I don't like your face!
(*Crosses to proscenium—stops.*)

STRAIGHT MAN. (*To* COMIC.) Now what have you done?
COMIC. She don't like my face.
STRAIGHT MAN. Is that really *your* face?
COMIC. It's nobody else's *but!*
STRAIGHT MAN. I suppose now I'll have to go fix it. Hold the car. (*Starts toward* TALKING LADY.)
COMIC. Hold it! *What are you doing?*
STRAIGHT MAN. What's the matter?
COMIC. You walked right through the motor!
STRAIGHT MAN. Oh, hell. Hold the car. (*Comes back—gets out between chairs—crosses to the* TALKING LADY.) Excuse me. On behalf of my friend and myself I wish to apologise for his behavior. You must forgive him his little eccentricities. Now please be a good sport and return with me to yon vehicle.
TALKING LADY. I ain't goin' noplace with that funny-lookin' *babboon!*
COMIC. (*Picking up chair to throw.*) I'll hit you in the head with this car in a minute!
STRAIGHT MAN. Watch it! You're spilling all the gasoline! (*Crossing to* COMIC.) Well, now you've done it. She won't be convinced.
COMIC. I'll convince her. Hold the car. (*Crosses to* TALKING LADY—*shouts.*) *Ya wanna eat?!*
TALKING LADY. *Yas!*
COMIC. Get in the car!

(TALKING LADY *and* COMIC *get in the car.*)

STRAIGHT MAN. *Here*—we go down the highway a hundred miles an hour. Beep! Beep! Where we going?
COMIC. Find a place to park the car and we'll buy a couple of beers.

TALKING LADY. Just a minute! Somebody's fooling with my leg!
COMIC. It's me and I ain't fooling.
TALKING LADY. My mother told me never to do anything like this.
COMIC. Hell, you ain't done nothin' yet.
TALKING LADY. If you ask me, you're fresh!
COMIC. If I ask you, I'm desperate.
TALKING LADY. Stop the car!
STRAIGHT MAN. E-e-eek!
COMIC. Wait a minute, don't go. Remember what Confuscious say: "Rape is impossible!"
TALKING LADY. Oh, really?
COMIC. "Woman can run faster with dress up than man can with pants down."
TALKING LADY. (*Getting out of car.*) Well, I never!
COMIC. Oh, go on, I'll bet you have.

(*The* TALKING LADY *crosses toward the wings, stops and turns.*)

TALKING LADY. In parting, I should like to make one brief comment. After listening to your asinine dialogue I have come to the conclusion that you two men are without a doubt the most insufferable specimens of humanity it has ever been my misfortune to encounter. Your illiteracy is appalling, your stupidity is monumental and if I were requested to express my superlative intelligence in describing my impression of your ridiculous existence I would be forced to unhesitatingly ask why you besmirch this grand and glorious universe with your supercillious imbecility. And so I give you *that!* (*Throws left hip at them.*) And *that!* (*Throws right hip at them.*) And— (*Turns around and throws backside at them.*) —*that!* (*Holds.*)

Comic. (*Turning to* Straight Man, *pointing at* Talking Lady's *backside*.) Hey, ... ! I just found a place to park the car!

Talking Lady—Comic—Straight Man. (*Together.*) *Bl-l-lackout!*

NOTE:

So—
After World War I when prohibition was in full swing, law and order authorities were part of that *Human Condition* that took a hell of a beating from burlesque comics. It was easy to ridicule judges and police officers when the American public was making folk heros out of gangsters like John Dillinger, Al Capone, Baby Face Nelson, Pretty Boy Floyd, Bonnie Parker and Clyde Barrow and so forth. Somehow all that changed with the kidnapping of the Lindbergh baby in 1932. The same way violence in movies and T-V took something of a back seat after the Kennedy assassinations. For a while.

But prior to '32 most of the courtroom and police officer sketches had already been written and to laugh at authority figures had become an accepted part of burlesque humor.

So here come de judge! Here come de judge! Here come de judge!

ACT I   BURLESQUE HUMOR REVISITED   55

(STRAIGHT MAN *returns to his lectern and flips pages.* TALKING LADY *exits and* COMIC *moves chairs up out of the way.*)

STRAIGHT MAN. (*Looking around to forestall interruption.*) AFTER WORLD WAR ONE, WHEN PROHIBITION WAS IN FULL SWING, LAW AND ORDER AUTHORITIES WERE PART OF THAT HUMAN CONDITION THAT TOOK A HELL OF A BEATING FROM BURLESQUE COMICS.

COMIC. (*Bringing stool to down center.*) So here come de judge! Here come de judge! Here come de judge.

STRAIGHT MAN. Now just a minute, I'm not finished!

COMIC. (*Sitting on stool center.*) Oh, yes, you are. (*Pointing at* STRAIGHT MAN *warningly.*) Tell 'em!

STRAIGHT MAN. (*Reluctantly to Audience.*) Now we're going to ask *you* to go to work. Want you to imagine, if you will, that you see before you a court room. Night court. And I'm a policeman. I wear a policeman's uniform, policeman's cap—badge. And .... here, is in judge's robes and he sits at a judge's bench in night court. That's not too tough, is it? I'm a cop. He's a judge. So—

The Courtroom Scene

STRAIGHT MAN. Hear ye! Hear ye! Hear ye! Court is now in session. Know ye by these presence all men are created equal of the people, by the people, for the people signify by saying "Aye" the whole truth and nothing but the truth so help you See-e-e-*sar!* All rise!

COMIC. *Siddown!*

STRAIGHT MAN. Telephone, your honor.

COMIC. Shaddup! I know it's the telephone. (*Pantomime telephone.*) Hello, whatta ya want? What? You're having a riot up there? Why didn't you have your riot this afternoon when a couple o' my boys were up that way? No, I'm not sending anybody over there on a cold and bitter night like this. Have your lousy riots during nice weather. G'bye! (*Hangs up—to* STRAIGHT MAN.) Now listen, that was the Mayor.

STRAIGHT MAN. The *Mayor!*

COMIC. Will you shut up or do I lock you up? What are you, an echo? Awright. Now, the Mayor says this is the only police station night court that isn't making any money, so we better start showing a profit by the end of this month or he's going to close up this damn dump. Awright. Is there a case waiting?

STRAIGHT MAN. No, sir, I delivered it this morning.

COMIC. Did you put my share in my locker?

STRAIGHT MAN. Yes, your horseship.

COMIC. *What?!*

STRAIGTH MAN. I said, "Yes, your worship."

COMIC. That's what I thought you said.

STRAIGHT MAN. I put your share in your locker, your horror.

COMIC. My *what?*

STRAIGHT MAN. Your honor.

COMIC. 'S what I thought you said. Where'd you make the delivery?

STRAIGHT MAN. To the "Clogged Fork" Restaurant.

COMIC. Oh, yes. I know that place.

STRAIGHT MAN. It's not a bad hash house. Only one problem: No rest room.

COMIC. How uncanny. (*Beat.*) Boy, that one went over with a hush, didn't it?

(*The* TALKING LADY *irately stomps onstage.*)

TALKING LADY. How much longer am I going to be left cooling my heels in that detention tank? (*To* STRAIGHT MAN.) You arrested me—let's get on with my trial— (*To* COMIC, *finger pointed.*) —and then I'm going to sue you and this court for every nickel—
COMIC. Shaddup, you dumb broad!
TALKING LADY. (*Shocked and indignant.*) *Oh-h!*
COMIC. Oh, pardon me, madam, I thought you were my mother.
TALKING LADY. I couldn't be. I'm married.
COMIC. (*Big react.*) *Oh-h!* Oh, that did it! *Oh!* Oh, I'll get you for that! Awright, officer. What's the charge?
STRAIGHT MAN. Salt in her battery.
COMIC. What?
STRAIGHT MAN. I don't want to repeat it.
COMIC. Whose salt was in her battery?
STRAIGHT MAN. Felonious's.
COMIC. Oh, felonious assault.
STRAIGHT MAN. Yes, your horseship. (*Look from* COMIC.) Your worship.
COMIC. 'S what I thought you said. We will now hear from the defen-*dant!* (*To* TALKING LADY.) Were you the feloni*zer* or the feloni*zee?* Were you the one that was felon-*eed?* Oh, the hell with it. What's your name?
TALKING LADY. (*A loud shout.*) *Jane—Doe!!*

(COMIC *reacts, falls back off stool, picks it up to bash* TALKING LADY.)

Comic. I didn't hear that. What's your name?
Talking Lady. (*Softly.*) Jane Doe.
Comic. That's better. (*Having resumed seat.*) Where are you from?
Talking Lady. Schenectady.
Comic. How do you spell that?
Talking Lady. I just moved to Troy.
Comic. You're sure about that?
Talking Lady. I'm positive.
Comic. Tut, tut, tut. Never say you're positive. Anyone who says he's positive is crazy.
Talking Lady. Are you sure?
Comic. I'm positive. You may proceed.
Talking Lady. Well, your honor, I was walking down the street—
Comic. No crime there if you keep walking.
Talking Lady. —and I came to an alley. (*Pointing at* Straight Man.) Then that *fiend*—
Comic. Hut-hut-hut. No recriminations. Remember, he hasn't been convicted yet. But he will be. Proceed.
Talking Lady. As I was passing the alley he reached out and *grabbed* me!
Comic. He grabbed you in the alley?
Talking Lady. He dragged me into the alley. He strangled me. He tore off all my clothes. And then—I fainted.
Comic. The monster! (*To* Straight Man.) Why don't you ever take me along when you patrol these alleys? Order in the court! *Order!*
Straight Man. A short beer!
Comic. Shut your face! (*To* Talking Lady.) Go on, my dear. And then what?
Talking Lady. And when I came to—
Comic. When you came to—

TALKING LADY. It was right then and there I found out I'd *lost* it.

STRAIGHT MAN. You lost it before they built City Hall.

COMIC. Shaddup! (*To* TALKING LADY.) So, not only were you foully assaulted, you were also robbed?

TALKING LADY. (*Crying.*) Yes, your honor. I was robbed. Gone. Stolen.

COMIC. (*Comforting—patting fanny.*) There, there, there, you poor child—

TALKING LADY. (*Glancing at Judge's hand on fanny.*) Watch it with that hand, your honor.

COMIC. Oh, you don't have to worry about that hand, my dear. (*Holding up other hand.*) *That's* the hand you have to watch out for.

STRAIGHT MAN. Your honor, I *object!*

COMIC. Objection overruled! Just tell you story. And remember, I am *Justice!*

STRAIGHT MAN. Justice what?

COMIC. Just as good as you are. Proceed.

STRAIGHT MAN. I was passing this alley, your horseship—

COMIC. I'm going to hit you so hard on top of your head that you'll have to untie your shoe laces to see where you're going. Now go ahead.

STRAIGHT MAN. I was passing this alley—your worship—

COMIC. Better.

STRAIGHT MAN. Pounding my beat—

COMIC. Pounding your what?

STRAIGHT MAN. My beat.

COMIC. Oh.

STRAIGHT MAN. When I heard this woman in the alley calling for her father.

COMIC. She *was?*

STRAIGHT MAN. She kept calling and calling: "Oh, Daddy! Oh-h-h, Daddy! Oh-h-h—*Da-d-dy*—!

TALKING LADY. Your honor, I object! I was robbed and I want satisfaction!

COMIC. Daddy didn't satisfy you, huh? Young lady, do you realize that this man is an officer of the law? Sworn to protect the public and uphold the constitution? When you walk along the street and suddenly a crook jumps out from behind a clump of bushes to accost you—

STRAIGHT MAN. (*Aside to* TALKING LADY.) How much you-a cost?

TALKING LADY. Two dollars. Same as always.

COMIC. Quiet in the court! And pay the two dollars! (*To* STRAIGHT MAN.) So-o—you've taken to robbing ladies in the alley. What did you get? Her watch?

STRAIGHT MAN. No.

COMIC. Her money?

STRAIGHT MAN. No.

COMIC. Her purse?

STRAIGHT MAN. No.

COMIC. Well, if you didn't get her watch, her purse or her money—what did you get?

STRAIGHT MAN. (*Taking and holding up woman's panties from pocket.*) *These!*

TALKING LADY. (*React.*) *Ee-e-ek!*

COMIC. In the locker! In the locker! Put my share in my locker!

(TALKING LADY *"raves" to right.* STRAIGHT MAN *moves to left.* COMIC *takes from his pocket a gun which he fires many times into the air. At the same time he takes the stool and places it up center.*)

NOTE:

By now it should be fairly apparent that a big ingredient in burlesque comedy is the "zany" quality. Once one suspended one's disbelief, said to himself, "Oh, come on, that's impossible, improbable, couldn't happen—too much zany—," then the burlesque goer just settled back and had a good time.

I guess maybe the zaniest sketch ever done was "Crazy House." A little "black humor" before its time. It wasn't cruel and it was funny. The comic gets a job as a night watchman in a lunatic hospital and all night long the patients go in and out of his bedroom, harrassing and bedeviling him to distraction.

Actually, over the years, I've counted more than a dozen other sketches that follow that same pattern. Some of them take place in an overloaded hotel instead of a loony bin and they all usually incorporated a large cast of characters charging in and out.

The setting is the lobby of a hotel. Stage right is an imaginary room clerk's desk and left of center is a cot.

(STRAIGHT MAN *enters and moves to his lectern.*)

STRAIGHT MAN. (*Reading.*) A BIG INGREDIENT IN BURLESQUE COMEDY WAS *THE ZANY QUALITY*. ONCE ONE SUSPENDED ONE'S DISBELIEF—
COMIC. (*Bringing two chairs down left of center.*) The zaniest sketch ever done was "Crazy House." We're not going to do that one.
STRAIGHT MAN. (*Flustered—turning pages.*) ACTUALLY, OVER THE YEARS, I'VE COUNTED MORE THAN A DOZEN OTHER SKETCHES THAT FOLLOW THAT SAME PATTERN. SOME OF THEM TAKE PLACE IN AN OVERLOADED HOTEL INSTEAD OF IN A HOSPITAL.
COMIC. That's the one we're going to do.
TALKING LADY. (*Entering.*) You've probably noticed by now that we're making do with a small cast here.
COMIC. (*Amazed—to* STRAIGHT MAN.) No! I didn't notice that! Did you notice that?
STRAIGHT MAN. Go make an entrance. (COMIC *exits.*)
TALKING LADY. So ordinarily this scene might incorporate eight or ten people. The setting is the lobby of a hotel. Over here—is the room clerk's desk. And over here—is a cot. (*Bangs an imaginary bell on desk.*) Ding! Ding! (*Exits.*)

Cot in the Corridor

STRAIGHT MAN. (*At imaginary hotel desk.*) Wow! We're jammed to the rafters in this hotel tonight. Big convention in town and every single room is taken including the broom closet. But I've got one cot left here in the corridor and the next man who comes in, I'm going to rent him this cot right here in the hall.

COMIC. (*Entering.*) Have you planted enough exposition? (*To Audience.*) This is a cot in the hall—in the corridor. Okay?

STRAIGHT MAN. Ah, good evening, sir. Welcome to "Embracing Arms." You wish a room, sir?

COMIC. Yeah, that's right. I'm a vasoline salesman and I'd like to slip in somewhere.

STRAIGHT MAN. Oh, I am sorry, sir. We're all full up.

COMIC. Oh, p-shaw!

STRAIGHT MAN. With the exception of one very nice room.

COMIC. I'll take it. How much is it?

STRAIGHT MAN. That'll be two dollars a night or a dollar and a half a week.

COMIC. I'll take it for a night and pay you for a week.

STRAIGHT MAN. That'll be fine, sir. Now we run a quiet, respectable hotel here, sir. No-noise-allowed.

COMIC. Good, good, good. I'm dead tired and I need a full night's sleep. Rest and quiet, that's for me. Where's the room?

STRAIGHT MAN. Back up a little bit. (COMIC *steps back two steps.*) There. You're in the room.

COMIC. I'm still standing in the lobby!

STRAIGHT MAN. You're a guest here for only two minutes and already you're rebuilding my hotel? How do you like the decor? What do you think of the furniture?

COMIC. The what?

STRAIGHT MAN. (*Pointing to nothing.*) Take a look at that beautiful, overstuffed divan.

COMIC. Overstuffed? It looks damned undernourished to me. Say, tell me, you don't have any bedbugs, do you?

STRAIGHT MAN. Why, sir! We don't have a *single* bedbug in this entire hotel.

COMIC and STRAIGHT MAN. (*Together.*) They're all married and have large families.

STRAIGHT MAN. Well, I'll say good night then, sir. And remember, although we're a small hotel we do have class and distinction. You're certain to enjoy your stay here. Give our quaint, little hotel a chance and I'm sure we'll tickle your risibility.

COMIC. I'll see you later.

STRAIGHT MAN. Where you going?

COMIC. Ain't nobody going to tickle my—What did you say?

STRAIGHT MAN. Oh, by the way, before I forget, would you like to leave a wake-up call?

COMIC. Why, yes. Call me at eight o'clock.

STRAIGHT MAN. Oh, I am sorry, sir. We're all out of eight o'clock calls.

COMIC. Okay, call me twice at four o'clock. I can be just as nutty as you are.

STRAIGHT MAN. And so good night. Now if during the night you should happen to want anything—I—betcha.

COMIC. I betcha I don't get it. Right? Right.

STRAIGHT MAN. Good night. Good night. Now I've got my eye on you so don't-you-*pull*-anything.

COMIC. (*Take.*) Go on, get the hell out of here.

STRAIGHT MAN. And remember—a respectable hotel. *PEACE!!* and *QUIET!!*

COMIC. (*Falling off cot and grabbing ears.*) Hot dammit to hell! (STRAIGHT MAN *exits.*) Oh, am I tired. I gotta get a good night's sleep. I'll bet I can even sleep on this cot. Oh, yeah, here I go. Mister Sandman, open-de-door, I'se comin' in. Hot damn. (*Stretches out.*)

TALKING LADY. (*Enters—does a bump after each line.*) Oh, boy! I never had it! Oh, boy! I never had it! Oh, 'boy! I-nev-er-had-*it!* (*Exits same side she entered on.*)

COMIC. Well, you're in a damn good spot to get it! (*Pounds around—terribly upset.*) Manager! Manager! Landlord! Landlord!

STRAIGHT MAN. (*Entering.*) Here! Here! Here! Stop that! What's the trouble?

COMIC. What the hell was that? "Oh, boy, I never had it! Oh boy, I never had it!" What did she never had?

STRAIGHT MAN. A seat on the subway.

COMIC. *A seat on the subway!?*

STRAIGHT MAN. That's right, now get back into bed. (*Nance.*) Just wrap yourself up and go to sleep.

COMIC. Wrap myself up with what? The *floor?*

STRAIGHT MAN. G'night, dearie. And if, during the night, there's anything I can do-o—

COMIC. Get the hell out of here.

STRAIGHT MAN. And remember—*peace* and *quiet!*

COMIC. Peace and quiet.

STRAIGHT MAN. Good night, Arabella. (*Blows kiss and exits.*)

COMIC. Oh, I'm going to have trouble with her, I can see that right now. Well, hell, I'm so damn tired— I've *got* to get some *sleep!*

(TALKING LADY *enters, wild eyed and furtive. She sneaks across, close to* COMIC *and passes between the chairs.*)

TALKING LADY. *Hey!*
COMIC. What the hell! Come on, you walked right through my bed!
TALKING LADY. I know you. You're Mickey Mouse!
COMIC. That's right, I'm Mickey Mouse.
TALKING LADY. And you left home 'cause you found out your father was a *rat!* (*Laughs hysterically and runs off stage.*)
COMIC. Landlord! Landlord! Manager!
STRAIGHT MAN. (*Entering.*) Will you stop making all that noise! I can't get any sleep!
COMIC. Well, what the hell was that—? "You're Mickey Mouse and your father was a rat!" I want to get some sleep. I thought you said I could have peace and quiet. (*Starts crying.*)
STRAIGHT MAN. Shh, shh, shh! That's right, peace and quiet. Now stop crying. Go to bed and go to sleep. (*Nance.*) And remember—no pussyfooting!
COMIC. No what?
STRAIGHT MAN. No pussyfooting!
COMIC. (*Take to Audience.*) Unh-*unh!*
STRAIGHT MAN.
Roses are red, violets are blue.
La-de-dah, I love you.
COMIC.
Roses are red, violets are blue.
La-de-dah, I'm gonna kick hell outa you.
STRAIGHT MAN. Good night, Louise. (*Blows kiss and exits.*)
COMIC. What kind of a hotel is this, anyway? I *gotta* get some *sleep!*

TALKING LADY. (*Enters—bump and grind on each line.*) Oh, boy, I just had it! Oh, boy, I just had it!

COMIC. (*Jumping out of bed.*) You're gonna get it again and it won't be on a subway! (*Sees* TALKING LADY *stop—he stops.*) Damn, Sam—lookee there, not a bad hunk o' flunkin'!

TALKING LADY. *Shh-h!* Do you have a fairy godmother?

COMIC. No, but I got an uncle I'm not too sure of.

TALKING LADY. (*Taking* COMIC's *hand—leading him.*) Come on. (*They stop.*) Where are you taking me?

COMIC. *Me?*

TALKING LADY. Come in here. I've got a leak in my bathtub.

COMIC. Well, go ahead, it's your bathtub.

TALKING LADY. (*Announcing.*) Hey! I just went to a nudists' wedding. Everybody there was completely nude.

COMIC. How were you able to tell who was the groom?

TALKING LADY. That was kinda hard.

COMIC. I'll bet it was.

TALKING LADY. But it sure was easy to pick out the best man.

(TALKING LADY *and* COMIC *both laugh. They face each other.* TALKING LADY *sneezes.* COMIC *wipes his face.*)

COMIC. You're standing in a draft.

TALKING LADY. Ah-h,—ah-h,—ah-h-h— (*Covers face with hand.*) —choo-o-o!

COMIC. That's better. (TALKING LADY *wipes her hand*

on Comic's face. *To Audience*.) She *saved* it for me!

TALKING LADY. (*As she exits*.) Oh, Daddy, Daddy, Daddy!

COMIC. (*Scraping feet on floor*.) Here,—kitty, kitty, kitty!

STRAIGHT MAN. (*Entering*.) Here! Where are you going?

COMIC. I want to see if my key fits her lock.

STRAIGHT MAN. Don't follow her. Any man who follows after a loose woman is *weak!*

COMIC. And when I come back I'll be a damn sight weaker.

STRAIGHT MAN. A woman like that is terrible!

COMIC. She looked damn good to me.

STRAIGHT MAN. Listen! I want you to get back into bed now and go to *sleep!*

COMIC. Then get the hell out of here!

STRAIGHT MAN. Good night, Gwendolyn. (*Blows kiss*.)

COMIC. I better go get my brother. He don't give a damn what happens.

STRAIGHT MAN. (*Waving*.) Over the river! (*Exits*.)

COMIC. Slop in the sewer, you son of a biscuit.

(TALKING LADY *enters, runs to* COMIC *and stands close*.)

TALKING LADY. Oh, Doctor! Oh, Doctor!

COMIC. (*Looking at her chest*.) You have a very bad case of the mumps.

TALKING LADY. (*Grinding her torso sensuously*.) I've got a toothache. I've got a toothache.

COMIC. Boy, the roots sure go down a long way, don't they?

TALKING LADY. (*Whispering loudly.*) Have you got your *stethescope* with you?
COMIC. My what?
TALKING LADY. Have you got it with you?
COMIC. I try never to be without it.
TALKING LADY. Is it an old one or a new one?
COMIC. Not too old. Don't listen to rumors.
TALKING LADY. But you've had it for quite a while.
COMIC. All my life. (*Grabbing* TALKING LADY.) Come here, you she-mule, I'm gonna haul your ashes!
TALKING LADY. Help! Help!
COMIC. I don't need no help. (TALKING LADY *breaks away and exits.*) Hot dammit! You heat the radiator and then cut off the steam! Come back here!
STRAIGHT MAN. (*Entering.*) Here! Who gave you that idea?
COMIC. Nobody. It's my own idea.
STRAIGHT MAN. I have told you and told you this is a quiet, respectable hotel. I'm afraid I'll have to ask you to leave.
COMIC. Aw, I wasn't going to hurt the old bag.
STRAIGHT MAN. That's a lot of baloney.
COMIC. Yeah, and she damn near got it, too. Besides, I can't go now, I don't feel well.
STRAIGHT MAN. (*Solicitous.*) Aw. You don't?
COMIC. No, I don't. I don't feel well at all.
STRAIGHT MAN. Oh, what a shame. That's terrible. You know what I do when I don't feel well?
COMIC. No, what do you do?
STRAIGHT MAN. Well, I go home and tell my wife. And she fixes me a nice, hot bath. After she bathes me and dries me off she gives me a soothing, alcohol rubdown. Then she makes me get into bed, she gets in along side me and pretty soon I feel just fine. Why don't you try that?

Comic. Okay, I will. What time will your wife be home?
Bl-l—ackout!
Comic and Straight Man. *Bl-l—ackout!*

NOTE:

Would you be interested in knowing that that sketch, "Cot in the Corridor," also utilized parts of "Crazy House," "Room to Rent," "Four Doors," "Two Cots Scene," "Try to Get In Bit," "Doctor Plumber," "Nudist Reform," "Love Escorts," "From Wine to Water" and many others? You wouldn't? Okay, then I won't tell you.

(Talking Lady *enters and comes down center.*)

Talking Lady. Hey, fellas, we're about at the halfway point here, aren't we?
Comic. Yeah, just about.
Straight Man. (*Crossing to his lectern.*) Which is a good place for me to bring up the fact— (*Flips pages in notebook.*) Ah, here we are.
Comic. (*To* Talking Lady.) We still have four or five more wild sketches to go, right? "Schoolroom," "Niagara Falls," "Joe, the Bartender" and "Who's on First?"
Talking Lady. "Hollywood," too, if we want an encore.
Straight Man. But first, by way of introduction— (*Reading.*) BEFORE AMERICA BECAME SO PREDOMINANTLY INDUSTRIAL—
Talking Lady. (*To* Comic.) I think we could all use a bit of a break.

STRAIGHT MAN. ONE OF THOSE HUMAN CONDITIONS—

COMIC. (*To* TALKING LADY.) Good idea.

TALKING LADY. (*To Audience.*) Let's take a short intermission. We'll see you all back here in fifteen minutes.

STRAIGHT MAN. But wait a minute—I was just going into—

(TALKING LADY *and* COMIC *cross to* STRAIGHT MAN, *take him by the arms and lead him, protesting, off the stage.*)

NOTE:

A lot of fun was had in burlesque with the childhood scene, the formative years, the learning process. That's right, the school room. Everyone comprehended, recognized and maybe even personally identified with the student-teacher relationship. (Incidentally, the paper-bag-wrapped balloon that I refer to with which the Straight Man hits the Comic is, I'm sure you all know, what used to be "the bladder." In the old days it was made from the stomach lining or intestines of a goat and made a great, loud-popping "SPLAT!" when struck against the side of the Comic's head. Anyway, for some reason or another, the Health Department stepped in and put a stop to the use of a goat's insides for such a purpose.)

This might also be the place to say that some comics did some sketches better than others and those comics came to be identified with their own private specialties. "The Schoolroom Scene" was pretty much accepted as the personal property of Lou Costello although I, myself, have seen it done by Red Buttons and also by Joe Yule, Sr. Remember him? Mickey Rooney's father.

ACT TWO

(*The* STRAIGHT MAN *enters carrying an inflated balloon in a brown paper bag. He crosses to his lectern and flips pages. He smiles and reads.*)

STRAIGHT MAN. A LOT OF FUN WAS HAD IN BURLESQUE WITH THE CHILDHOOD SCENE, THE FORMATIVE YEARS, THE LEARNING PROCESS—
 TALKING LADY. (*Entering—crossing down to chairs.*) The schoolroom!
 STRAIGHT MAN. (*Reading a beat late.*) —THE SCHOOLROOM. YES, EVERYONE COMPREHENDED, RECOGNIZED AND MAYBE EVEN PERSONALLY IDENTIFIED—
 COMIC. (*Entering carrying his ice pick—starts to skip, dance and sing.*) "School days! School Days!—
 TALKING LADY. (*Joining in singing and dancing.*) "Dear old Golden Rule days—
 COMIC and TALKING LADY. (*Together.*)
"Readin' and writin' and 'rithmatic—
 Taught to the tune of a hickory stick—"
 STRAIGHT MAN. Oh, the hell with it! (*Crosses down to set-up chairs and dancing "students."*)

The Schoolroom Scene

STRAIGHT MAN. (*Herding students to seats.*) All right, students, come along. Recess is over. Take your seats. Hurry along now. Good morning, students!
 TALKING LADY and COMIC. Good morning, teacher!

(COMIC *takes from his pocket an ice pick which he shows to the* TALKING LADY.)

COMIC. Hey! Look what I found in the school yard.
TALKING LADY. An ice pick!
COMIC. Yeah! You get the ice and with this ice pick I'll come over to your house and we'll have us a *par-tee!* (*Prances around—giggles—to Audience.*) I'm a ba-a-a-ad-d boy!
STRAIGHT MAN. All right, sit down, children. Johnny. Mary. Now this morning we're going to take up poetry.
COMIC. (*Sitting in "front" chair stage center.*) Up your poetry.
STRAIGHT MAN. What was that?
COMIC. I said, "I love poetry."

(STRAIGHT MAN *hits* COMIC *with bag-wrapped balloon.*)

STRAIGHT MAN. Stand up and say a poem. (COMIC *stands and faces Audience.*)
COMIC.
"Pumpkin pie and sassafrass,
 She walked in the ocean clear up to her ankles."
   (*Sits.*)
STRAIGHT MAN. No. That's not a poem.
COMIC. Wait 'til the tide comes in. (STRAIGHT MAN *hits* COMIC *with bag.*)
STRAIGHT MAN. Mary, come down here and recite a poem for us.

(TALKING LADY *and* COMIC *exchange seats. As she passes, he waves the ice pick at her threateningly. She dodges.*)

TALKING LADY.
We had a cat down on our farm
Who swallowed a ball of yarn;
And when this cat had kittens,
They all had sweaters on.

(COMIC *takes stage and reacts with indignant disbelief.*)

COMIC. Oh, no! Oh, for Pete's sake! What the hell kind of a poem is that? I never heard anything so awful in my whole life! (*Big melee.* STRAIGHT MAN *hits* COMIC *with balloon when he passes.* COMIC *threatens* TALKING LADY *with ice pick as she moves to go back to the "second" chair.* COMIC *to* TALKING LADY *behind his seat.*) Hey, come on over to my house tonight for a goose dinner. I'll bring the *finger!*
STRAIGHT MAN. Stop that! You're so smart; do you have a better poem?
COMIC. *Yes!* (*Faces Audience.*)
Damon and Pythias—they ran around.
Wherever Damon went—Pythias was found.
One night Pythias called Damon a skunk,
So Damon went out and got Pythias drunk.
(*Sits, pleased, in "first" chair.*)

(TALKING LADY *throws arms in air and stomps around in a silent "outrage" take.*)

STRAIGHT MAN. (*Shaking his head sadly.*) Brushing up on your ignorance again, I see.
COMIC. (*Waving ice pick at* TALKING LADY.) Get the hell out of here!
TALKING LADY. Watch it! Watch it!
COMIC. Go on! I won't hurt you.

TALKING LADY. That's what a guy said to my sister and now she can't button her coat! (*Holds up hand to* STRAIGHT MAN.) Teacher! Teacher! I've got one.

COMIC. (*Moving back to "second" chair.*) You'd be in lousy shape without one.

STRAIGHT MAN. Yes, Mary. You say you have one?

TALKING LADY. Just a little one. (COMIC *guffaws loudly.*)

STRAIGHT MAN. Now stop that! (*To* TALKING LADY.) All right, Mary, let's see it. (*Big reaction* COMIC *and* TALKING LADY.) I *mean*—let's hear it.

TALKING LADY.
I love you strong, I love you mighty,
I love your jammies next to my nightie.
Don't get excited, don't be misled,
I mean on the clothesline, not in the bed.
    (*Sits.*)

COMIC. (*Big reaction—in simulated pain.*) Oh-h-h! That is so *old!* That is the oldest— (*Waves ice pack at* TALKING LADY.) I should—I oughta—

TALKING LADY. Look out!

(TALKING LADY *moves back to "second" chair.* COMIC *steps to center to recite.*)

COMIC. That's even older than, "There was an old hermit named Dave—"

STRAIGHT MAN. (*Hitting* COMIC *with balloon-bag.*) Now, enough of that—behave yourself! Coming in here with those limericks. All right, Johnny, it's your turn. Let's see you do better.

COMIC. (*Talking very fast.*) A cockroach has no politics—

STRAIGHT MAN. Hold it! Hold it! Hold it! Why so fast? Slow it down. Try it again.

COMIC. (*Very slowly.*) A—cock-roach—has—no politics—

STRAIGHT MAN. Come on, come on—not that slow. Not too slow. Not too fast. Just sort of half-fast. (*Big reaction from all three.* STRAIGHT MAN *hits* COMIC *with bag-balloon.*) Say the poem!
COMIC.
A cockroach has no politics,
He does not care for fame.
He has no right to be in your soup,
But he gets there just the same.
 (*Sits.*)
TALKING LADY. Byukk! That's sick! That's disgusting! (*Taking stage—raving around.*) That makes me want to toss my cookies all over the—
COMIC. Aw, go home and wash your neck! (*Retreats to "second" chair.*)
TALKING LADY. (*Waving hand in air.*) My turn, teacher!
STRAIGHT MAN. All right, Mary.
TALKING LADY. (*Facing front.*)
A farmer went to a burlesque show,
He got a seat in the very first row.
A girl came out and did her dance;
Zip! went the buttons off his vest."
 (*Sits—beat—to* STRAIGHT MAN.)
That's prose, teacher.
COMIC. (*Big to-do.*) I don't believe it! I don't believe it! I'll kill her! I'll club her to death! I'll slice her up into little—An axe! An axe! Where can I find an axe?
TALKING LADY. (*Moving back to "second" chair.*) Don't axe me!
COMIC. Oh, no! Oh, no! (*Waves ice pick at* TALKING LADY—*turns to* STRAIGHT MAN, *hand up.*) Hey, teach, I got a riddle!
STRAIGHT MAN. Okay, let's hear it.
COMIC. What is it has three legs, flies in the air like

a horse, but ain't, carries a bottle of ketchup balanced on his head and bats left-handed?

STRAIGHT MAN. Wow! What has three legs, flies in the air—like a *horse*—?

COMIC. But ain't.

STRAIGHT MAN. —carries a bottle of ketchup balanced on his head and bats left-handed?

COMIC. Yeah, what is it?

STRAIGHT MAN. I don't know. What is it?

COMIC. I don't know either, but boy, I make up some tough ones, don't I?

(COMIC *laughs.* STRAIGHT MAN *hits him with the bagged balloon.* COMIC *falls back to "second" chair.* TALKING LADY *moves to "first."*)

STRAIGHT MAN. Get the hell out of here! Mary, come up to the front of the class. Now I'm going to ask you a biblical question.

TALKING LADY. A what?

STRAIGHT MAN. A biblical question. Out of the bible. (COMIC *is waving his ice pick at the* TALKING LADY *and she dodges.*) Now, Johnny, you stop that! Leave her alone. (COMIC *subsides—tentatively.*) Now pay attention, Mary. What was the first thing Eve said to Adam after they came out of the Garden of Eden?

(COMIC *brandishes ice pick.* TALKING LADY *whirls on him.*)

TALKING LADY. Don't you stick that damn thing in me!

TALKING LADY—COMIC—STRAIGHT MAN. (*Together.*) Bl-l—ackout!

NOTE:

Lets now go into what was commonly known in burlesque as *The Rave*. As earlier mentioned, burlesque performers loved to get dramatic. Well, a *Rave* is when a performer gets his teeth into a dramatic bit, tears up the scenery, rants and raves and explodes all over the stage in wild histrionic fervor and then *raves* himself or herself off stage and usually to thunderous applause.

Many famous sketches fall into the category of frustration and rave. Off-hand I can think of such burlesque stalwarts as "The Imaginary Husband," "Pork Chops," "Doctor Mantell," "Joe, the Bartender," "Niagara Falls" (you know—"slow-w-ly I turned—!") and many, many variations and combinations thereof. I'll give you a couple short versions. I'll start off with "Niagara Falls" and then fall into a piece of "Joe, the Bartender."

(STRAIGHT MAN, *at lectern, begins to read.*)

STRAIGHT MAN. FRUSTRATION. THE COMIC IN A QUANDARY. THIS WAS ONE OF THE MOST POPULAR CATAGORIES OF BURLESQUE HUMOR AND BURLESQUE SKETCHES. HOW MANY OF YOU HAVE HEARD OF OR MAYBE SEEN THE CLASSIC SKETCH, "FLUGLE STREET?"

(*The* TALKING LADY *enters and goes to the chairs up stage.*)

TALKING LADY. IS THIS THE SPOT WHERE YOU TALK ABOUT "FLUGLE STREET" AND HOW BURLESQUE PERFORMERS LOVED TO GET DRAMATIC? (*Brings chairs down to left of center, sets them together side by side.*)
STRAIGHT MAN. OVER-DRAMATIC.
TALKING LADY. AND THEN YOU DESCRIBE WHAT IS A "RAVE" SKETCH AND YOU NAME SOME OLD CLASSICS AND THEN WE DO ONE.
STRAIGHT MAN. WELL, YEAH, SORT OF.
TALKING LADY. COME OVER HERE. SIT DOWN.
STRAIGHT MAN. (*Coming to* TALKING LADY *and chairs.*) WELL, WAIT A MINUTE, WHAT ABOUT—

Niagara Falls

TALKING LADY. (*Pushing* STRAIGHT MAN *down onto a chair.*) The scene—a park bench—in a park. (TALKING LADY *turns and exits.* COMIC *enters and speaks front.*)

ACT II   BURLESQUE HUMOR REVISITED   81

COMIC. Cheese and crackers, what a dead town. I never *saw* so many people looking so *sad!* They're all like a bunch of dentists,—always looking down in the mouth. (*Laughs, turns and spies* STRAIGHT MAN.) Look at the *puss* on that guy! Hey, Mister, what makes you look so sad? Maybe I can help you.

STRAIGHT MAN. (*Looking up—very dramatic.*) *You ask me why I'm sad!* (*Approaches* COMIC.)

COMIC. (*Jumping back.*) What the hell is that? Yes. I ask you, "Why are you so sad?"

STRAIGHT MAN. You are the first person who ever spoke kindly to me. You look like a man with a kind face. Yes. Yes. A kind face!

COMIC. (*Aside.*) What the hell am I getting into here?

STRAIGHT MAN. (*Taking* COMIC *down stage.*) Come over here. I promised I'd never tell this to a living, breathing human being—so you listen.

COMIC. Aw, come on!

STRAIGHT MAN. (*Dramatically.*) I wasn't always a slimy, scurvy bum—like you. I came from a fine family. I was well bred and raised in the best tradition. I had a good education. I went off to fight for my country. Do you see *that?* (*Bares chest—*COMIC *looks closely.*) A *bullet hole!*

COMIC. It's moving.

STRAIGHT MAN. I marched home again and went into business. I worked hard and diligently and with moderate success. Then I met her. She was a beautiful flower blooming in the garden of youth. We fell in love and were married. After two glorious years of ecstatic bliss and happiness, the good Lord blessed us with a beautiful pink and white bouncing baby boy. (*Cries.*) We were *very happy!* My whole life, my entire existence was wrapped up in my darling wife and child. And then *he*—came back into my life. My best friend. He had saved my life overseas and here he was, broken in health and in spirit. I welcomed him into my family. I fed him. I clothed him. I set him up in business. I bid him make *my* home *his* home.

COMIC. (*Nadding*.) So he sold it.

STRAIGHT MAN. Then one day I received a telegram telling me I had to go to San Francisco on business. It was a big deal and could mean great success. So I bid my darling wife and baby goodbye and asked my best friend to take good care of them until I returned.

COMIC. Oh, oh, oh, you should'na done that.

STRAIGHT MAN. After a month of hard but fruitful work, I returned. I hurried home to tell my darling wife of my great success. I opened the door and no one was home. A note on the table was from my wife. I opened it with trembling fingers. In it she said she did not love me any more and had gone away with our baby—and my best friend. *I swore revenge!* I threw over my business. Sold everything I owned. And started on a quest to find that man who had wrecked my home. The search lasted for years. It destroyed my health and took every cent I owned. I was two weeks behind them in Galveston, Texas where they boarded a steamship for South America. A week behind them in Rio de Janiero. Five days behind them at the Cape of Good Hope in South Africa. Three days at Madagascar. Twelve hours at Singapore—

COMIC. He moves fast.

STRAIGHT MAN. And *finally*—at the gates of Calcutta—!

COMIC. Ah—*hah!*

STRAIGHT MAN. I saw him.

COMIC. Good boy!

STRAIGHT MAN. The sun beat down with intense

heat. Just as I was about to spring upon him—my weakened condition, aggravated by the pitiless rays of the tropical sun, caused me to *fall*—in a *heap*—on the sands at his feet. And when I regained consciousness—he was gone.

Comic. Hot-dammit to hell!

Straight Man. So the search began anew.

Comic. Hey, you don't give up, do you?

Straight Man. Two years!

Comic. Oh, hell.

Straight Man. Fruitless!

Comic. My God!

Straight Man. And then one day—

Comic. *Yes?!*

Straight Man. —at the brink of *Niagara Falls*—I found him. The man who had ruined my life. Who stole my wife and baby. I saw him standing there and with all my anger pent up inside, I saw red. Slow-w-ly I turned. Step by step—inch by inch—I crept upon him. And when I got close enough I grabbed him by the throat—and I choked him— (*Beats up on* Comic.) —and I hit him and strangled and bit and kicked and— (Comic *is on the floor*—Straight Man *suddenly comes out of it.*) Oh! What are you doing down there?

Comic. *I'm waiting for a streetcar!* (*Screaming and struggling to his feet.*) What the hell's the *matter* with you? You don't have to get so carried away! You're crazy, Mister!

Straight Man. I'm sorry! I'm sorry! Oh, *what* have I *done!?*

Comic. What have you *done?* I'll *tell* you what you've done! Don't you know what you just done—to *me?* You kicked me and strangled me! I ask you why you look so sad and you go into a—screaming and hollering—*Take it easy!*

STRAIGHT MAN. Please forgive me. I don't know what happened, I—I guess I forgot myself.

COMIC. I'd rather you'd forget *me!* You come at me like—Well—That's all right. I guess I understand. You've had quite a horrible time. I can see how you'd get carried away. Whew! So what happened?

STRAIGHT MAN. To what?

COMIC. To the guy.

STRAIGHT MAN. What guy?

COMIC. The guy at Niagara Falls.

STRAIGHT MAN. *Niagara Falls!* There he stood. The lust for his blood welled up in me. I saw red. Slow-w-ly I turned!

COMIC. Now be careful.

STRAIGHT MAN. Step by step—inch by inch—

COMIC. Watch out, now—

STRAIGHT MAN. Then I grabbed him and I pounded him and beat on him and— (COMIC *is on the floor.*) —kicked him and scratched and punched and tore at his throat until I—

COMIC. *Hey-y-y!*

STRAIGHT MAN. Oh! Oh, what—oh, for heaven's sake, look what I've done. Oh, you poor man, let me help you up. I'm so sorry—

COMIC. (*Getting up onto his feet.*) Get *away* from me! Don't you touch me! You're balmy, Mister! They oughta lock you up! You're a *menace!* A guy can't even say two simple words like Nia— (*Stops suddenly—take—laughs to Audience.*) That was close, wasn't it?

STRAIGHT MAN. What was?

COMIC. *That* was. Me. I almost forgot myself and said Niagara Falls and then you'd—
STRAIGHT MAN. *Niagara Falls!*
COMIC. Oh, hell!
STRAIGHT MAN. Slow-wly I turned.
COMIC. Oh, God—!
STRAIGHT MAN. Step by step—inch by inch—
COMIC. (*Lying down on floor.*) Okay, I'm down. I'm already down. You don't have to—
STRAIGHT MAN. And I jumped on him and pounded him and kicked and gouged and fought and—!
COMIC. All right! All right! All right! *Hey-y-y!* (*Jumps up onto feet—angry.*) Get away from here! Go on, get out of here!
STRAIGHT MAN. Oh, I'm so sorry. I don't know what comes over me. Please forgive me.
COMIC. I forgive you! I forgive you! Just beat it—go on—get *out!* (STRAIGHT MAN *exits shaking head—begging* COMIC'S *pardon.*) Cheese and crackers! Guy's a *nut!* (*Sits on bench—brushes self off.* TALKING LADY *enters, sees* COMIC, *walks straight to him and stares.*) What the hell are you looking at?
TALKING LADY. (*Big.*) Oh, you *poor,* poor man! *Why* do you look so *sad?*
COMIC. (*Big take.*) Unh-huh-hu-huh-nn— (*Waving front row of Audience back.*) You better move back a few rows. I don't want you to get splashed with all the blood. (*To* TALKING LADY.) *You ask me why I look so sad!!* Pull up a park bench, little girl, my tail will touch your heart. (*Waves hips.*) I used to be happy. Yes, I was. Happy as if I were in my right mind. I had a happy, pink wife and we had a happy, pink, bouncing, baby boy that we used to bounce around the house like a volley ball. He was born on the Pennsylvania Turnpike so we named him Toll

Booth. Then *he* came into my life. He was busted in health and in spirit but he had a lot of schmaltz and moxie and I fed him and clothed him and set him up in business and that's just what he gave me.

Talking Lady. What?

Comic. The business. I came back from San Francisco, found a note from my wife: "I've just run off with your best friend, you poor sap, don't you ever listen to soap operas on the radio?" I swore I'd get revenge! I chased them all-l over the world. South America. Africa. Madagascar. I chased 'em through the cotton fields of Alaska. I was breathing down their necks in Singapore and finally, in the black hole of *Calcutta*—I—*lost* him! (*Beat—looks back at* Talking Lady.) That's supposed to upset you.

Talking Lady. Hanh?

Comic. Say, "Oh, dear" or something.

Talking Lady. Oh, dear.

Comic. That's got it. Stay away from that black hole of Calcutta. And *finally*—!

Talking Lady. (*Stands up.*) Oh, thank God!

Comic. Atta girl! Very good. I found him! Yes! I saw red. My anger was all pent up or—something. Don't you want to know where it was?

Talking Lady. Hanh?

Comic. Go ahead. Go ahead, ask me where it was I found him. What a minute. Stand over here. Now hold that. (*Positions* Talking Lady, *then himself.*) Um, good. Oh-h, you're gonna *love* this. Now—go ahead and ask me where we were when I found him.

Talking Lady. Well, yes, I was wondering, during all your pursuits, where it was you might eventually arrive at the time you encountered the man you were after. In fact—

COMIC. Look, don't editorialize. Don't pad your part. Just ask me—simple—*where*.
TALKING LADY. All right, where were you?
COMIC. Where were we? You ask me where we were? I'll tell you where were we! There I saw him standing at the brink of *Niagara Falls*—!
STRAIGHT MAN. (*Dashing on stage.*) *Ni-a-gara Fall-l-ls—!!* Slow-w-ly I turned—!
COMIC. Oh, no! Oh, no! (*To* TALKING LADY.) Come on, little girl, we better get the hell *out* of here!

(COMIC *grabs* TALKING LADY'S *hand and pulls her off stage as* STRAIGHT MAN *exaggeratedly stalks them, arms waving, in a "Rave."* STRAIGHT MAN *turns and moves to the two chairs which he picks up to place up stage out of the way.*)

NOTE:

Incidentally, one of those *Human Conditions* that burlesque loved to ridicule and make fun of was our universal appreciation of fantasy. Most animated cartoons, in a world of fantasy, as you know, drip with burlesque humor. Slapstick, zany, the be-set upon underdog comic. And fantasy brings me to "Joe, the Bartender" and that *rave* I was telling you about.

The stage, you have to understand, is absolutely and completely empty. After "Joe" gets "shot," stage lights go out and the Talking Lady is centered in a bright, green spotlight. She exits, stage lights up, and then the Comic does his burlesque impression of everything he has just seen which, naturally, includes the green spotlight. Okay?

STRAIGHT MAN. PLAYING ON AUDIENCE'S UNIVERSAL APPRECIATION OF FANTASY, BURLESQUE PERFORMERS USED TO DO A SCENE CALLED "JOE, THE BARTENDER." AND THAT BRINGS ME TO THAT *"RAVE"* I WANTED TO TELL YOU ABOUT. A "RAVE" IS WHEN—

(*The* TALKING LADY *enters followed by the* COMIC *and they immediately go right into the scene.*)

TALKING LADY. Come on, come on, come on, come on.—(Etc.)
STRAIGHT MAN. (*Annoyed and frustrated.*) OH, FOR HEAVENS SAKE! (*Exits other side.*)

Joe the Bartender

(*The* TALKING LADY *enters followed by the* COMIC. *They move to down center.*)

TALKING LADY. Come on, come on, come on, come on. Quit dragging you feet. Shake a leg. Let's go, let's go.
COMIC. Where we going anyway? You said you'd take me to a speakeasy where we could get a drink.
TALKING LADY. That's where we're going. That's exactly where we're going.
COMIC. How far is it?
TALKING LADY. From here? About twenty blocks.
COMIC. Twenty blocks!
TALKING LADY. We can walk it in an hour. If we ride it will take two hours.

COMIC. Then let's walk, I'm thirsty. (*They walk in a small circle.*)
TALKING LADY. Well, here we are.
COMIC. (*Take.*) Where?
TALKING LADY. At the speakeasy.
COMIC. (*Looking around.*) That was twenty blocks?
TALKING LADY. Yup.
COMIC. In an hour?
TALKING LADY. Come on, let's go in.
COMIC. I gotta do something about this damn watch.
TALKING LADY. Watch out for these swinging doors. (COMIC *winces, ducks and feels around but can't find the doors.* TALKING LADY *knocks a secret knock on another invisible door.* COMIC *tries to see.*) Oh, hi, Jim, it's me. Oh, it's okay, he's a friend of mine. Thanks, Jim. (*To* COMIC.) Come on, let's go. Well, here we are.
COMIC. Where we are?
TALKING LADY. In the speakeasy.
COMIC. We're in the speakeasy now?
TALKING LADY. Certainly, that's right.
COMIC. Looks like the same damn place we started from to me.
TALKING LADY. What's the matter with you, are you crazy?
COMIC. Not yet but I expect to be very soon, thank you very much. Hey-y—damn good camouflage. Must be tough as hell on the cops raiding a place like this.
TALKING LADY. (*Foot and elbow up.*) Come on, belly up to the bar.
COMIC. Belly up to what bar?
TALKING LADY. This bar. This bar right here. (COMIC *sees* TALKING LADY *with her foot up as if on bar rail. He tries to do the same lean and nearly falls over.*) Oh, Hiya, Joe. Joe, I want you to meet a friend

of mine. (*To* Comic.) This is my pal, Joe, the bartender. We grew up together. Went to school together. Go on, shake hands with Joe.

Comic. Joe who?

Talking Lady. Joe Small.

Comic. So damn small I can't even see him.

Talking Lady. Say hello to Joe.

Comic. (*Shaking an invisible hand.*) Hello, Joe.

Talking Lady. No, not down there. He's a big guy.

Comic. (*Wipes hand—shakes higher.*) Hello, Joe.

Talking Lady. What's that, Joe? Why, yes, thanks. We'll have a couple of beers.

Comic. Make mine a short beer. (Comic *watches* Talking Lady *blow off foam, drink beer and wipe her mouth.* Comic *picks up a beer he doesn't have.*) Lips to lips—gums to gums—look out stomach—here she comes. (*Puts "beer holding" hand up to mouth, on across face and brushes back hair.*)

Talking Lady. Hey, thanks, Joe, that's good beer. (*To* Comic.) Isn't it? How'd you like the beer?

Comic. Oh, good! Great beer, Joe! Thanks a lot. (*Turns away—arms up and down.*) What the hell's the matter with me? (*Looks back to* Talking Lady.) Hey!

Talking Lady. Yeah?

Comic. Don't look now—I mean, I don't want to start anything but he forgot to give me my change.

Talking Lady. No, he didn't. It's right there.

Comic. It is? (*Looks at nothing.*) Well, what the hell—keep the change, Joe.

Talking Lady. Hey, what a sport! That's terrific. A nine and a half dollar tip!

Comic. What?! Gimme that! (*Grabs for money—struggles to find bills along bar—doesn't.*) Well, easy come, easy go.

TALKING LADY. What's that, Joe? You want us to have a drink on the house?

COMIC. It's about time.

TALKING LADY. Me? Oh, I'll have another short beer, Joe. (*To* COMIC.) What about you?

COMIC. Oh, hell, make mine a big one.

TALKING LADY. All right, fine. What's that you say, Joe? You *will?* Hey, that's terrific! (*To* COMIC.) Look, see what he's pulling down.

COMIC. (*React.*) I'm afraid to look. What—what's he pulling down?

TALKING LADY. That big mug there. That big beer stein. Looks like a goldfish bowl on a glass stem, doesn't it?

COMIC. Yeah. Yeah, that's what it looks like all right.

TALKING LADY. What's it look like?

COMIC. Huh?

TALKING LADY. I say, what's it look like?

COMIC. A—a goldfish bowl on a glass stem.

TALKING LADY. (*Delighted.*) That's *right!* That's exactly what it looks like. You know, for a minute there I was afraid maybe you couldn't see it— (*To "Joe."*) What's that, Joe? Say, that's terrific. (*To* COMIC.) Joe says it holds almost a gallon and he's filling it up with good, cold beer just for you. (*To "Joe."*) Say, Joe, thanks. Hey, that's a beautiful hunk of antique crystal. It has? You don't say!

COMIC. I know he didn't say 'cause I didn't hear a damn thing.

TALKING LADY. (*To* COMIC.) Joe just told me that that big glass cost five hundred dollars, that it's been in his family for three generations and is impossible to replace.

Comic. Go on, I got a whole house full of 'em! Just like that one.

Talking Lady. Well, thanks, Joe. Oh, we'll be careful. (*To* Comic.) Okay, drink up. Well, go ahead.

Comic. I did. I just finished it. (*Gulps—wipes mouth.*)

Talking Lady. How could you finish it; it's still sitting right there?

Comic. It is, huh?

Talking Lady. Well, go on, drink it. You don't want to insult Joe.

Comic. *Oh, hell no!*

Talking Lady. Now be careful. Be careful with that glass.

Comic. (*Lifting.*) Have I got it?

Talking Lady. Yeah, you got it. Watch out, you're sloshing it.

Comic. I am?

Talking Lady. Look out! Be careful! Don't drop it, it cost $500.00!

(Comic *staggers back and forth, pretending to drink and trying to keep his balance.*)

Comic. It's heavy!

Talking Lady. I'll bet it is.

Comic. (*Suddenly stopping and looking up.*) Just what the *hell* have you got me *doing* here? (*Throws up hands and puts them on his hips.*) Acting like an idiot—!

(Talking Lady *suddenly jumps back, stamps her feet and goes into shock. Off stage sound effect of tremendous crash.* Comic *falls back in wide-eyed puzzlement.*)

TALKING LADY. *Aggh-h-h!* Oh, my *God!*
COMIC Oh, my *goodness!*
TALKING LADY. *Look* what you've done!
COMIC. Look, look, looky what I done did!
TALKING LADY. Five hundred dollars worth of antique crystal, handed down from generation to generation—
COMIC. I just handed it down for the last time.
TALKING LADY. (*Very excited—talking fast.*) Pick it up! Pick it up! Pick up the pieces! Put them in your hat! (*Pushes* COMIC *onto his knees.*)
COMIC. In your hat—
TALKING LADY. Get that piece over there. Watch out, you're getting beer all over your trousers.
COMIC. You're making a damn fool out of me!
TALKING LADY. What's that, Joe? Joe, I'm sorry. I'm sorry he did that. It was an accident.
COMIC. Hell, could happen to anybody.
TALKING LADY. What's that? Oh, *sure!* Well, of *course* we'll make it good, Joe!
COMIC. Why, hell, *yes!*
TALKING LADY. Yes, I *know.* Five hundred dollars. (*To* COMIC.) Give me five hundred dollars, quick!
COMIC. There.
TALKING LADY. Come on, come on, hurry up.
COMIC. (*Slapping imaginary money on bar.*) I just *gave* you! One, two, three, four, five—hundred bucks —right there. I can be just as nutty as you are.
TALKING LADY. You fool! This is no time to be kidding around! Can't you see he's getting *angry?*
COMIC. (*Snapping finger.*) So what?
TALKING LADY. What's that, Joe? Joe—Joe, don't pull that gun. Don't pull that gun, Joe, it might go off. If you pull that gun, I'll have to pull mine. Look

out, Joe! Joe, *don't!* Don't make me do it, Joe! (*Gun shot from off stage.*) *Aah-h-i-i-e-e-e!!*

COMIC. Let's go home. Come on, let's go home.

TALKING LADY. Oh, my God, what have I done? Look what I've done! Oh, what have I done? (*Into big "rave"—tears, etc.*) Oh, Joe, Joe, I'm sorry, I didn't mean to do it. I didn't mean to do it, Joe. I didn't mean it. Please forgive me, Joe. Joe, you forced me to do it. Speak to me, Joe.—What's that? *Dead! Agg-h-h-h!* It can't be! Not dead! Can't be dead! Close your eyes, Joe, don't stare at me that way. Oh, look at all the blood. All over the floor. Joe's blood. Joe, my friend. We went to school together. We grew up together. Ladies and gentlemen of the jury, it was an *accident!* What's that, your honor? Oh, *no! Guilty!* Murder in the first degree! The cell! The bars! And now—it's time. Oh, Joe—Joe, don't let them do it! Not up those thirteen steps! Stop them, Joe! I don't want to be hanged until dead! Please, Joe! They're putting the rope around my neck, Joe! The trap is about to be sprung! The rope is tighter! Tighter! Stop them, Joe! I don't want to die! I'm too young to die! Don't let me die, Joe! I don't want to *die-e-e!* I'm—too—*young-g—*to—*di-e-e-e!* (*Exits raving.*)

COMIC. (*React.*) *What—the—hell—was that?!* (*Repeats and burlesques everything previous with lots hocum.*) Hm-m! Round and round—twenty blocks in one hour—*Zip!* "Here we *are?*" Watch out for them swinging doors, they'll slap you right in your aspirin tablets. *Hello, Joe!* How's about a short beer? How's about a *long* beer? How's about a *tall* beer in a short glass? What's that? I insulted you? Oh, I insulted your *goldfish* bowl. I didn't insult it, I *knocked* it over! (*Swipes arm across "bar"—jumps back.*) *Agh!* Don't

ACT II   BURLESQUE HUMOR REVISITED   95

you pull that gun on me, you son-of-a-gun. That's no way to get your gun off. I mean, that gun might go off. Then I'll pull mine! Take *that!* (*Nothing—glances toward wings.*) And *that!* And that and that and *that!* (*Nothing—looks off stage—gives up.*) All right then, I'll pull my knife and I'll *stab* you! (*Gun shot from off stage.*) *Agg-h-h-h-ee-ei-i!* (*Big geshrei.*) What have I done? What have I done? I killed my best friend! Don't look at me like that, Joe! Close your eyes, you're dead, you dumb dodo! (*Looks at floor—screams.*) *Bee-lood!* (*Lifts pants—up to tiptoes.*) *Agh!* They're taking me away! The courtroom! The trial! I'm *not guilty!* I'm *not!* I'm *not!* I'm not guilty! Soap on my neck—*rope* around my neck. I'm not guilty! *Keep that trap closed!* Joe! Don't let 'em do it to me, Joe! I don't want to die, Joe! I'm too young to die, Joe, I'm too young—to—di-i-e-e—! (*To Audience.*) Hey, this scene is more fun than that *Niagara Falls*—

STRAIGHT MAN. (*Off stage.*) *Ni-i-a-a-gar-a Fa-a-all-ls!!* (*Jumps on stage.*) Slow-w-ly I turn-n-ed—!

COMIC. Oh, no! Oh,—get the hell out of here! (*Makes retreating swipes at* STRAIGHT MAN *who stalks him and chases him off.*)

(STRAIGHT MAN *moves over to his lectern, turns a few pages and opens his mouth to speak.* TALKING LADY *steps down stage and says to the Audience:*)

TALKING LADY. Back in the thirties—Bud Abbott and Lou Costello!

(TALKING LADY *turns up left and exits.* STRAIGHT MAN, *hung up, turns to watch her go, his mouth hanging open.* COMIC, *right, enters and moves to down center where* STRAIGHT MAN *has to join him.*)

NOTE:

Remember back in the beginning when I told you about Weber and Fields' play-on-words, their supposed confusion and mis-interpretations of the language and how these comedy ingredients created frustration and anguish on the part of the poor, be-set upon, nebish comedian? This turned out to be a basic foundation for an awful lot of burlesque humor. Get the comic up a tree, throw rocks at him, drive him up a frustration wall and yet, never fear, he almost always comes out a winner in the end.

With Weber and Fields and performers like them, burlesque comedy was, for a long time, clean and home-spun—based on misinterpretation, the play-on-words and frustration. For example, following this same formula, back in the thirties we had—

Bud Abbott and Lou Costello!

Who's On First

Comic. (*Over his shoulder to* Straight Man.) Excuse me.

Straight Man. (*Reluctantly coming down.*) Why? What did you do?

Comic. Huh? No, you don't understand. I'm looking for the manager of this ball team. Are you the manager?

Straight Man. Why, yes, I'm the manager of this ball club.

Comic. Oh, fine. Well, I'm the new rookie.

Straight Man. (*Shaking hands.*) Hey, welcome. We've been looking for you.

Comic. Oh, thank you. You know, I was just shaggin' some flies with some of the players out there on the field and I was having a tough time because I don't know any of the player's names. So I was thinkin', you bein' the manager and all, you could maybe tell me the players' names so's I'd know their names when I play ball with 'em and all.

Straight Man. Why, certainly. Glad to help you out there. The men don't have ordinary names, you know. We call them by nicknames.

Comic. Oh, you mean like Dizzy and Daffy?

Straight Man. Yeah, that's right.

Comic. Oh, I have a nickname.

Straight Man. You do? What is it?

Comic. Dopey.

Straight Man. Dopey. That's a pretty good name. Throw the ball to Dopey. Yeah, I like that.

Comic. Yeah, well, anyway—so if you could tell me

the names of all the players so I could say hello to the boys when—

STRAIGHT MAN. Why, of course, be a pleasure. As I say—nicknames. Now let's see, we have Who on first, What's on second and third base, I Don't Know.

COMIC. That's exactly what I want to find out—the names of all the players so I call 'em by name—you know, when I talk to 'em.

STRAIGHT MAN. That's what I'm telling you. Who's on first, What's on second and third base, I Don't Know.

COMIC. Look, come over here. I'm afraid you don't understand me. See, I just want to know the names of all the players so I—

STRAIGHT MAN. That's what I'm telling you.

COMIC. Tell you what, let's take one player at a time.

STRAIGHT MAN. All right, fine.

COMIC. You got a first baseman?

STRAIGHT MAN. Yes, of course we have a first baseman.

COMIC. Tell me the name of the guy playing first base.

STRAIGHT MAN. Who.

COMIC. The man on first base.

STRAIGHT MAN. Who.

COMIC. The fella playing first base.

STRAIGHT MAN. Who.

COMIC. The *guy* on *first base!*

STRAIGHT MAN. Who.

COMIC. Look, I'm asking you who!

STRAIGHT MAN. And I'm telling you. Who.

COMIC. You're not telling me, you're asking me. I just want to know—*what* is the man's name on first?

STRAIGHT MAN. No, What's on second.

COMIC. I'm not asking you who's on second.
STRAIGHT MAN. Who's on first.
COMIC. (*Shrug.*) I don't know.
STRAIGHT MAN. Third base.
COMIC. How did we get to third base?
STRAIGHT MAN. You just happened to mention his name.
COMIC. Well, if I just happened to mention his name, *who* did I say was playing third base?
STRAIGHT MAN. No, Who's playing first base.
COMIC. I'm not asking you who's on first!
STRAIGHT MAN. Well, he is.
COMIC. Who is?
STRAIGHT MAN. Yes!
COMIC. What's his name?
STRAIGHT MAN. What's on second.
COMIC. Who's on second?
STRAIGHT MAN. Who's on first.
COMIC. I don't know.
COMIC and STRAIGHT MAN. Third base.
COMIC. We're back to third base. Look, you got a first baseman? You know the first baseman?
STRAIGHT MAN. I know him very well.
COMIC. Okay. You're the manager.
STRAIGHT MAN. I'm the manager.
COMIC. You pay the man a salary.
STRAIGHT MAN. Certainly do, every week.
COMIC. Now, when the man comes down to get paid, —who—gets the money?
STRAIGHT MAN. Every dollar of it.
COMIC. Hah-hah!—Well, who gets it?
STRAIGHT MAN. Of course he does.
COMIC. Who does?
STRAIGHT MAN. Certainly. He's entitled to it.
COMIC. Who is?

STRAIGHT MAN. Absolutely. He's worked hard for it. Oh, sometimes his wife comes down to pick it up for him.

COMIC. *Who's wife?!?*

STRAIGHT MAN. Yes!

COMIC. Look, what's the man's name who gets the money?

STRAIGHT MAN. No, no, What gets second base's money.

COMIC. I'm not talking about who's on second!

STRAIGHT MAN. Who's on first.

COMIC. I don't know.

COMIC and STRAIGHT MAN. Third base.

COMIC. Look, forget the infield, all right?

STRAIGHT MAN. All right.

COMIC. Okay. Now,—you got an outfield.

STRAIGHT MAN. Of course we have an outfield.

COMIC. Tell me the left fielder's name.

STRAIGHT MAN. Why.

COMIC. I just thought I'd ask.

STRAIGHT MAN. I just thought I'd tell you.

COMIC. Okay, tell me the left fielder's name.

STRAIGHT MAN. Why.

COMIC. Because!

STRAIGHT MAN. No, he's the center fielder. You see, you know these players' names as well as I do. Coming out here and asking—

COMIC. (*Overlapping.*) I don't even know what the hell I said here! All I want to know is *what* is the left fielder's name?

STRAIGHT MAN. No, no, What is on second base.

COMIC. Will you stay out of the *infield!*

STRAIGHT MAN. All right, now, take it easy.

COMIC. Okay, you don't want to tell me the left fielder's name,—forget it. All right now?

STRAIGHT MAN. All right.
COMIC. Okay. You got a pitcher?
STRAIGHT MAN. Of course we have a pitcher. What kind of a ball club would this be without a pitcher?
COMIC. All right. Tell me the pitcher's name.
STRAIGHT MAN. Tomorrow.
COMIC. What time?
STRAIGHT MAN. What time what?
COMIC. What time tomorrow you gonna tell me *who* is pitching?
STRAIGHT MAN. Who is not pitching. Who is—
COMIC. If you say first base I'm going to give you such a smash in the—
STRAIGHT MAN. Now be careful now.
COMIC. I don't know why you're making it so tough. I have to know these things. See, I'm a catcher—
STRAIGHT MAN. I know that.
COMIC. And I'm a pretty good catcher, too.
STRAIGHT MAN. I'm glad to hear that.
COMIC. Lemme give you a for instance. Now I'm behind the plate. A guy comes up to bat and he *bunts* the ball—
STRAIGHT MAN. You get busy.
COMIC. So being a good catcher, I want to throw the man out at first base.
STRAIGHT MAN. Certainly do.
COMIC. So I flip off my mask, run up, pick up the ball—and I throw it—to *who?*
STRAIGHT MAN. That's the first thing you've said right all day.
COMIC. I don't even know what the hell I said here. So I pick up the ball and throw it to *who?*
STRAIGHT MAN. Naturally.
COMIC. Oh, *Naturally!* I throw the ball to Naturally and then he—

STRAIGHT MAN. No, no,—you don't throw the ball to Naturally! You pick up the ball and you throw it to *Who!*
COMIC. Naturally.
STRAIGHT MAN. There you go.
COMIC. Same damn thing! I throw the ball to—I tell you this: I throw the ball, somebody better be there! And whether it's Who or What or Naturally or Why— And to tell you the truth, I don't give a damn!
STRAIGHT MAN. Oh, he's the short stop!
COMIC. (*Storming off.*) Oh, nuts!
STRAIGHT MAN. No, he's the bat boy!
COMIC. Oh, go to hell!!
STRAIGHT MAN. He's the owner of the club. Say, you know these players' names as well as—

(COMIC *raves off left.* STRAIGHT MAN *stops at his lectern and flips pages.*)

NOTE:

Now this following sketch, "Hollywood," is not to be confused with the classic, "Stand In." I'll save that one for Volume II of "Burlesque Humor Revisited." No, this one is an amalgamation of quite a few sketches like "Poo Poo Choo Choo," "Scrutinize," "Indian Scene," "Dirty Story," "Moving Picture," "Archibald," "Fire," "Title" and a few more. And what we have here might be considered something of an encore to the others, a sort of summing up of the ingredients that comprise burlesque humor. And from this it's possible to see how burlesque comedy could go beyond the risque and into the dirty. What a shame, too.

ENCORE

(*The Straight Man moves left to his lectern.*)

Straight Man. (*Reading.*) AND GRADUALLY BURLESQUE HUMOR, AS YOU CAN SEE, GOT MORE AND MORE RISQUE, MORE AND MORE SUGGESTIVE. AND, UNFORTUNATELY, THIS STARTED TO HAVE A DETRIMENTAL EFFECT ON THE NUMBER OF BURLESQUE FANS.

Comic. (*Entering.*) Hold it, hold it, hold it. What are you telling us? These sketches were written when?

Straight Man. I'll say before 1940.

Comic. And this is 1974. With today's permissiveness and openness, are you asking an audience like this to believe that burlesque might have become—what—too naughty?

Straight Man. Not really. But take for instance our next scene. If it's done well—in good taste—

Comic. Look, let's just do it and find out. (*Pointing to Audience.*) Let *them* tell *you*.

Straight Man. Check! Meet you 'round the corner—in a half an hour.

(Straight Man *and* Comic *exit opposite sides.* Talking Lady *enters and comes down to the lectern left. She looks over her shoulder, flips pages and then reads:*)

Talking Lady. HERE'S A LITTLE-KNOWN FACT ABOUT BURLESQUE SKETCHES AS THEY USED TO BE DONE IN THE OLD DAYS.

A LOT OF TIMES, FOR ONE REASON OR ANOTHER, THE STAGE MANAGER OF A BURLEY SHOW WOULD FIND IT NECESSARY TO CHANGE THE RUNDOWN OF A SHOW QUITE SUDDENLY AND WITHOUT NOTICE. SO WHOEVER CAME OUT ON STAGE WOULD FIRST TURN AND LOOK AT WHATEVER BACKDROP HAD BEEN LOWERED AND THAT WOULD TELL HIM WHICH OR WHAT SCENE HAD BEEN SET IN THIS SLOT. SAY THE SCENIC DROP SHOWED A FOUNTAIN IN A EUROPEAN-TYPE PLAZA. THE STRAIGHT MAN WOULD COME OUT AND SAY, "WELL, HERE I AM IN— (*Turns and looks behind her.*) —SUNNY SPAIN." THEN THE COMIC WOULD COME OUT AND THEY WOULD DO "THE BULLFIGHT SCENE." OR, SAY, TALL BUILDINGS, "WELL, HERE WE ARE IN—TIMES SQUARE."

STRAIGHT MAN. (*Entering.*) Hey, come on! Now you're doing my lecture. I'm the one supposed to say—

TALKING LADY. You don't need to, I just did. (*To Audience.*) OR MAYBE THE DROP WOULD BE THE PAINTED REPLICA OF THE FRONT OF GRAUMAN'S CHINESE THEATRE—

(*Indicates to* STRAIGHT MAN, *"Take it away, chum" and exits left.* STRAIGHT MAN *reacts with a deep breath and a sigh.*)

Hollywood

STRAIGHT MAN. Well, here we are in— (*Turns and looks behind.*) —Hollywood. And I'm ready to shoot my new movie. But I still don't have a leading man. (*The* COMIC *enters and crosses stage.*) However, I put an ad in the paper— (*Watches* COMIC *pass and start to leave.*) Hey! Where you going, Elmer?

COMIC. (*Stopping.*) How'd you know my name was Elmer?

STRAIGHT MAN. I just guessed it.

COMIC. Then guess where the hell I'm going.

STRAIGHT MAN. Now stop that. Come back here.

COMIC. Hey! You the guy put an ad in the paper for a leading man actor?

STRAIGHT MAN. That's right, I'm the guy!

COMIC. Okay, let's go, I take the job. Where's the stage and what's the play?

STRAIGHT MAN. Take it easy, you haven't got the job yet. And it's not a play, it's a movie. But first I have to interview you. Stand there, I want to scrutinize you.

COMIC. Get the hell out of here!

STRAIGHT MAN. Come back here!

COMIC. You lay one hand on me—! This is Hollywood, right? The land of the fruits and the nuts. I may be nuts but *you*—ho, ho, ho.

STRAIGHT MAN. Be quiet. I have to ask you some questions. How old are you?

COMIC. Thirty-six years old.

STRAIGHT MAN. How long you been out of work?

COMIC. Thirty-six years.

STRAIGHT MAN. How long were you in your last place?

COMIC. Twelve months.

STRAIGHT MAN. What did you do?

COMIC. Twelve months.

STRAIGHT MAN. One of the parts I have open—

COMIC. How's that?

STRAIGHT MAN. I say, one of the roles—I have open

—in this movie—is the part of a French lady's escort. You know what is an escort?

Comic. Well, of course.

Straight Man. Give me a sentence using the word, "escort."

Comic. I was climbing over a barbed wire fence and I got my escort.

Straight Man. No, no, no, no. I'm afraid you'll never make an actor.

Comic. I'd rather make an actress.

Straight Man. Say, wait a minute—On second thought, possibly you can help me in another area. You know, being a motion picture director I receive hundreds of applications from beautiful women every day. Now you know I can't handle all those women.

Comic. Hundreds of women a day?

Straight Man. That's right.

Comic. Break your damn back.

Straight Man. So that's where you come in.

Comic. Hey, I like this job.

Straight Man. Now let's organize this.

Comic. Good idea. Where's the bedroom? I'll organize 'em 'til their teeth rattle.

Straight Man. Now stop that! There is no bedroom, now come on! Now I'll be over here. And when a young lady comes in, you stand her over there while I scrutinize her.

Comic. (*Take.*) From there?

Straight Man. Of course.

Comic. Standing up?

Straight Man. Certainly.

Comic. Betcha ten dollars. *This* I gotta see.

Straight Man. What's the matter with you? I can scrutinize a girl from clear across the street.

Comic. The hell you say!

STRAIGHT MAN. That's nothing. Why, I've seen my father scrutinize girls around corners.

COMIC. Around *corners!*

STRAIGHT MAN. And you should know my uncle—

COMIC. Never mind your uncle, your father's enough for me.

STRAIGHT MAN. Now be sure that when you stand the girl over there you don't get between us. I would hate to have to scrutinize her *right through you!*

COMIC. (*Jumping aside.*) Hot dammit to hell!

STRAIGHT MAN. Now when a woman comes in I'll give you a cue.

COMIC. No, thanks, I'll use my own cue.

STRAIGHT MAN. I mean I'll give you a signal.

COMIC. Oh, a signal. Hey, just a second—before we go any further. How much am I being paid for this job?

STRAIGHT MAN. I'll pay you what you're worth.

COMIC. Oh, hell, I ain't working *that* cheap!

STRAIGHT MAN. And just you remember one thing: I'm your boss.

COMIC. You're my boss. And what am I?

STRAIGHT MAN. You are nothing.

COMIC. Hey, that's a great job you got—boss over nothing. (*Bowing low—mock subservience.*) Yes, boss. Yes, Master. Yes, you go to hell. (*Starting to leave, turns back.*) Oh, come on, why can't I be your leading man actor?

STRAIGHT MAN. Well, I don't know, I suppose I could try you out.

COMIC. (*Holding up a finger.*) Now be careful there.

STRAIGHT MAN. Will you stop that! Now pay attention while I set this scene.

COMIC. Right! Set the scene.

STRAIGHT MAN. Let us say that you are walking

down the street. A beautiful, French damsel gets out of her car and starts to go into a saloon. You've seen a saloon?

COMIC. I—think so. (*Mugs.*)

STRAIGHT MAN. And she drops her handkerchief.

COMIC. Ah! Gives me a great opportunity to seduce myself to her.

STRAIGHT MAN. Yeah, you go seduce yourself. Now you run around the car.

COMIC. I run around the car.

STRAIGHT MAN. You pick up the handkerchief.

COMIC. I pick up the handkerchief.

STRAIGHT MAN. And just as she's going through the swinging doors into the saloon—you *give* it to her!

COMIC. On the fly.

STRAIGHT MAN. No, she'll stop long enough for you to give it to her.

COMIC. She'll have to or she ain't gonna get it.

STRAIGHT MAN. Now the camera is right behind you.

COMIC. How close behind?

STRAIGHT MAN. Pretty close. After all, he has to focus.

COMIC. Bo'f us? (COMIC *and* STRAIGHT MAN *are standing side by side.* STRAIGHT MAN *is amused by* COMIC's *last question and he pats* COMIC's *hip affectionately.* COMIC *looks down.* STRAIGHT MAN *does it again.*) Stop that. Don't do that.

STRAIGHT MAN. Why not?

COMIC. Because I don't like it.

STRAIGHT MAN. Then you do it to me. I *love* it!

COMIC. (*Pushing* STRAIGHT MAN.) Get the hell out of here.

STRAIGHT MAN. Now come on. You're playing the part of a fireman and you're going to save a young woman.

Comic. Oh, I already did that.
Straight Man. You did? Who did you save?
Comic. I saved a young girl. Don't tell me you didn't read about it. Did you see this morning's paper?
Straight Man. No, what was in it?
Comic. My lunch.
Straight Man. No, come on. *You* saved a young girl?
Comic. Oh, hell yes. Last Saturday night I met two pretty girls—a blonde and a brunette. They both wanted to go out with me. So I saved the blonde for Tuesday.
Straight Man. All right, now cut the foolishness. You're playing the part of a fireman—named Archibald.
Comic. Hey, that's a hot role!
Straight Man. You're darned right. Now— (*Pointing.*) —over here is a ten story building and it's on fire. It's burning down.
Comic. Where?
Straight Man. Right there. Don't you see it?
Comic. Oh, sure, I see it. Come on.
Straight Man. Where we going?
Comic. Observation ward.
Straight Man. Now come on! And on the top floor of this burning, ten-story building is our beautiful, French, damsel. Remember? From the car?
Comic. Oh, yes, I gave it to her in the saloon.
Straight Man. Her handkerchief.
Comic. Of course. What else?
Straight Man. Now beneath our beautiful, French damsel the building is on fire and she's trapped.
Comic. A regular towering inferno.
Straight Man. You might say that.
Comic. I do and I get sued.

STRAIGHT MAN. Then don't say it. Now you are a fireman. Your name—

(*The* TALKING LADY *enters and stands at proscenium looking around. The* COMIC *sees her and reacts.*)

COMIC. Excuse me, boss, I think I hear my mother calling me. (*Crosses to* TALKING LADY—*suave.*) Hello, there.

TALKING LADY. (*To* COMIC—*French accent.*) Excuse, please. I look for zee movie director?

COMIC. And you have come to the right place. Stand right there, I'll fix you up. I mean, I'll fix it up. (*Crosses to* STRAIGHT MAN.) Okay, boss, there she is, all ready to be interviewed and scrutinized. Go ahead, I call your bluff. Let me see you *scrutinize* her.

STRAIGHT MAN. What's the matter with you? I've been scrutinizing her ever since she walked over here.

COMIC. Already? What the hey!

STRAIGHT MAN. Why, I've scrutinized her three or four times.

COMIC. (*To* TALKING LADY.) How'd you like it?

TALKING LADY. Par-don, monsieur?

COMIC. (*To* STRAIGHT MAN.) Hey-y, did you hear that?

STRAIGHT MAN. She's French.

COMIC. Yeah-h? (*To* TALKING LADY.) You say you're a moving picture actress?

TALKING LADY. Mais, oui. Mais oui.

COMIC. We may. We may. But first we have to ask you a few questions. Tell me—

STRAIGHT MAN. Hold it! *I* will ask the questions.

COMIC. That's what I said. Go ahead.

STRAIGHT MAN. Mam'selle, how do you do? I am the director of this epic.

Comic. *Epic!?*

Straight Man. And allow me to introduce you to my assistant.

Talking Lady. Enchante, monsieur.

Comic. You do and you'll clean it up.

Straight Man. He is also applying for the job of your new leading man.

Talking Lady. Ah-h, cheri! I *love* zee leading man! (*Holds* Comic *sideways and rubs his chest.*) Zee leading man, he is always so sex-ee! He is so wonderful!

Comic. Make a bigger circle!

Talking Lady. (*Puckering up.*) Ah, mon cheri, you kiss me, yes?

Comic. (*Breaking away.*) Get the hell out of here!

Straight Man. Here, here, here. What's the trouble?

Comic. I'm not going to kiss her "yes" or anything else. What the hell is this?

Straight Man. Stop that! Come over here. Now listen to me. You're handling this situation all wrong.

Comic. I didn't lay a finger on her!

Straight Man. You've got to remember, she's a foreigner and a glamorous actress. She's got *"it"!*

Comic. Well, I've got *"if."*

Straight Man. *"If"?*

Comic. *If* she wants any more of *"it,"* I'll be glad to help her out.

Straight Man. No, no, no, that's not what I'm talking about. Now look here, you just met this lady. She doesn't know you.

Comic. Well, I don't know her. I'm taking as big a chance as she is.

Straight Man. Now listen to me. With a lady like that you know you've got to use charm, be continental. You've got to be soft.

Comic. Hell, it ain't no good that way.

STRAIGHT MAN. Now look, you tip your hat; you nod your head and grasp her digits.
COMIC. She'll have me arrested. Grab her what?
STRAIGHT MAN. Her digits. Press them firmly.
COMIC. Press 'em, hell, I'll hang my hat on 'em.
STRAIGHT MAN. And after you shake her digits—
COMIC. She gives me—a bust—in the mouth. I hope. Wait a minute. You mean to tell me she's going to stand for all that? Grabbing her digits?
STRAIGHT MAN. Of course. She'll love it.
COMIC. Well, okay, if you say so. (*To* TALKING LADY.) 'Scuse me, I have to grab your—I'm supposed to press your—

(*Flustered,* COMIC *raises his hands while staring at* TALKING LADY's *chest. She jumps back in shock.*)
TALKING LADY. Oh-h! How dare you, monsieur! I have nevair been so insult in my life! (*Waves hips and does a bump.*) I like—zat!
COMIC. (*Emulating her—bumps twice.*) So do I, kid. Want to lock bumpers?
TALKING LADY. (*Winding up with a slow grind.*) Oh, yes, monsieur?
COMIC. Set that thing for nine o'clock and I'll move in. (*Suddenly moving to and addressing a man in the front row.*) Why don't you look at me some time?
TALKING LADY. (*Bumping to the right and left sides.*) Zis for you. Zat for you. (*Big bump to the front.*) And zat for your old man!
COMIC. (*Watching "it go," peering and pointing up to the balcony.*) It's a high fly into left center field—!
STRAIGHT MAN. Will you stop that!
COMIC. My old man gets the best of everything. Did you see that, boss? She tried to bump me off!
STRAIGHT MAN. Come on! Come on! Will you two

stop it! Now let's get on with making this movie. All right. Now, mam'selle, you are on top of this burning building—right here. (*To* COMIC.) And you—are Archibald, the fireman, and you enter.

COMIC. Oh, I'll slip in there somewhere.

STRAIGHT MAN. All right,—*action!*

TALKING LADY. Archibald! Archibald! Save me! Save me!

(COMIC *runs to wings and staggers back to on stage "carrying" and balancing a long, imaginary board.*)

STRAIGHT MAN. Here, here, here. What's all this? What are you *doing?*

COMIC. I'm carrying this long—ten story board— over to this burning building. And then I'm going to—

STRAIGHT MAN. What? Where in the *hell* are you ever going to get a *ten story board?*

COMIC. Same place you got the burning building. So I lean it up against the burning building so she can slide down, into my arms and—

STRAIGHT MAN. Hold it! Hold it! That would never work. She can't slide down a board. She's a woman of pride and personality.

COMIC. Oh, I didn't kno-o-ow that. You're right, it wouldn't work.

STRAIGHT MAN. Of course not.

COMIC. If the board had a nail in it it would tear her pride and rip hell out of her personality. I'll tell you what: I'll throw up a rope. She can tie it around her waist and I'll *pull* her down.

STRAIGHT MAN. You fool! That would disarrange her phisiognomy!

COMIC. It would bust *hell* out of it!

TALKING LADY. Archibald! Archibald! Save me! Save me!

COMIC. (*Applauding.*) Hey! Very good. (*To* STRAIGHT MAN.) She's a great actress.

STRAIGHT MAN. Very talented.

COMIC. She deserves an Oscar for this performance. (*Looks down into trousers.*) Right, Oscar?

STRAIGHT MAN. All right, never mind. Now she's down, she's safe—we'll work out the details when we shoot it—and she's grateful, she wants to thank you. And now we go into the love scene.

COMIC. (*Grabbing* TALKING LADY *from behind and hugging her tightly.*) Hot damn! Come here, Frenchy!

STRAIGHT MAN. Here, here, here! What the hell are you doing? Does Ronald Coleman make love like that?

COMIC. No, but Rin Tin Tin does.

TALKING LADY. (*Turning on* COMIC.) Par-don, monsieur, have you evair been in zee movie before?

COMIC. Oh, hell, yes. I was in "The Millionaire's Daughter and the Butcher Boy."

TALKING LADY. Ah? What part did you play?

COMIC. I delivered the meat.

TALKING LADY. Oh, a small role, eh? (*Flounces away.*)

COMIC. I'll kick the she-lack out of you!

STRAIGHT MAN. Come on, come on. Now the young lady is thanking you and you— (*Spitting the "p"s.*) —you say something appropriate to her.

COMIC. (*Wiping an eye.*) What?

STRAIGHT MAN. I say, you say something appropriate.

COMIC. (*To* TALKING LADY.) Gimme a towel. Okay, okay, something appropriate. (*Romantically to* TALKING LADY.) Oh, darling, my darling, I love you. To show you how much I love you I'm going to buy you a beautiful pair of silk pajamas. On one leg will be embroidered, "Merry Christmas." On the other leg will be embroidered, "Happy New Year." And I just hope, my darling, that you'll invite me to drop in between the holidays.

TALKING LADY—COMIC—STRAIGHT MAN. (*Together.*) *Bl-l-l-ackout!*

(STRAIGHT MAN *returns to lectern.* COMIC *and* TALKING LADY *drift up toward him.*)

STRAIGHT MAN. (*Turning pages to end.*) So now we ask you—has burlesque humor died?

COMIC. Hell, no. The original concepts and basic formula of burlesque comedy will be with us forever.

STRAIGHT MAN. (*Reading.*) JUST FROM THESE SAMPLE EXAMPLES OF OLD-STYLE BURLESQUE SKETCHES IT'S EASY TO SEE HOW A GREAT PERCENTAGE OF OUR PRESENT-DAY T-V, STAGE, SCREEN AND NIGHT CLUB HUMOR PERTAINS AND DRAWS HEAVILY ON THE SATIRE AND THE RIDICULE GAGGED UP ON THE BURLESQUE STAGES OF MANY YEARS AGO.

TALKING LADY. Redd Foxx of "Sanford and Son" is a pure, baggy-pants comic, right out of burlesque.

COMIC. Why, almost every routine Milton Berle, Jerry Lewis, Mel Brooks, Woody Allen and dozens of other comedians do pays great tribute to the old-style burlesque humor, if not actually to out-and-out burlesque training itself.

STRAIGHT MAN. (*To Audience.*) Sure wish I could

have given you my lecture. See, — it tells about how, in the history of—

TALKING LADY. *(To Audience.)* Thank you. And good night.

STRAIGHT MAN. No, but wait a minute—

TALKING LADY. *(To* COMIC.*)* Ready? — *Go!*

COMIC and TALKING LADY. *(In unison.)* Ni-a-ga-ra Fa-a-l-lls!! *(Toward* STRAIGHT MAN.*)* Slo-o-owly — I — tur-r-rned—!! *(Chase* STRAIGHT MAN *off.)*

CURTAIN

THREE MUSKETEERS
Ken Ludwig

All Groups / Adventure / 8m, 4f (doubling) / Unit sets
This adaptation is based on the timeless swashbuckler by Alexandre Dumas, a tale of heroism, treachery, close escapes and above all, honor. The story, set in 1625, begins with d'Artagnan who sets off for Paris in search of adventure. Along with d'Artagnan goes Sabine, his sister, the quintessential tomboy. Sent with d'Artagnan to attend a convent school in Paris, she poses as a young man – d'Artagnan's servant – and quickly becomes entangled in her brother's adventures. Soon after reaching Paris, d'Artagnan encounters the greatest heroes of the day, Athos, Porthos and Aramis, the famous musketeers; d'Artagnan joins forces with his heroes to defend the honor of the Queen of France. In so doing, he finds himself in opposition to the most dangerous man in Europe, Cardinal Richelieu. Even more deadly is the infamous Countess de Winter, known as Milady, who will stop at nothing to revenge herself on d'Artagnan – and Sabine – for their meddlesome behavior. Little does Milady know that the young girl she scorns, Sabine, will ultimately save the day.

SAMUELFRENCH.COM

NO SEX PLEASE, WE'RE BRITISH
Anthony Marriott and Alistair Foot

Farce / 7 m., 3 f. / Int.

A young bride who lives above a bank with her husband who is the assistant manager, innocently sends a mail order off for some Scandinavian glassware. What comes is Scandinavian pornography. The plot revolves around what is to be done with the veritable floods of pornography, photographs, books, films and eventually girls that threaten to engulf this happy couple. The matter is considerably complicated by the man's mother, his boss, a visiting bank inspector, a police superintendent and a muddled friend who does everything wrong in his reluctant efforts to set everything right, all of which works up to a hilarious ending of closed or slamming doors. This farce ran in London over eight years and also delighted Broadway audiences.

"Titillating and topical."
- "NBC TV"

"A really funny Broadway show."
- "ABC TV"

SAMUELFRENCH.COM

www.ingramcontent.com/pod-product-compliance
Lightning Source LLC
Chambersburg PA
CBHW070644300426
44111CB00013B/2255